AROUND

washington

WITH KIDS

by Kathryn McKay

Fodor's Travel Publications
New York • Toronto • London • Sydney • Auckland

www.fodors.com

CREDITS

Writer: Kathryn McKay

Series Editors: Karen Cure, Caroline Haberfeld
Editor: Andrea Lehman
Editorial Production: Linda Schmidt
Production/Manufacturing: Robert Shields

Design: Fabrizio La Rocca, *creative director*;
Tigist Getachew, *art director*
Illustration and Series Design: Rico Lins, Keren Ora
Admoni/Rico Lins Studio

ABOUT THE WRITER

Each month writer Kathryn McKay scours the D.C. area with
her two young children in tow researching her column, "In
Our Own Backyard," for *Washington Parent* magazine.

Fodor's Around Washington, D.C. with Kids

First Edition
ISBN 0-679-00492-0
ISSN 1526-1980

Important Tip

Although all prices, opening times, and other details in this
book are based on information supplied to us at press time,
changes occur all the time in the travel world, and Fodor's
cannot accept responsibility for facts that become outdated
or for inadvertent errors or omissions. So always confirm
information when it matters, especially if you're making a
detour to visit a specific place.

Special Sales

Fodor's Travel Publications are available at special discounts for bulk purchases for sales promotions or premi-
ums. Special editions, including personalized covers,
excerpts of existing guides, and corporate imprints, can be
created in large quantities for special needs. For more infor-
mation, contact your local bookseller or Special Markets,
Fodor's Travel Publications, 201 E. 50th Street, New York,
NY 10022. Inquiries from Canada should be directed to your
local Canadian bookseller or sent to Random House of
Canada, Ltd., Marketing Dept., 2775 Matheson Boulevard
East, Mississauga, Ontario L4W 4P7. Inquiries from the
United Kingdom should be sent to Fodor's Travel
Publications, 20 Vauxhall Bridge Road, London, England
SW1V 2SA.

PRINTED IN THE UNITED STATES OF AMERICA
10 9 8 7 6 5 4 3 2 1

CONTENTS

WELCOME TO GREAT DAYS!

Between pick-ups, drop-offs, and after-school activities, organizing a family's schedule is one full-time job. Planning for some fun time together shouldn't be another. That's where this book helps out. In creating it, our parent-experts have done all the legwork, so you don't have to. Open to any page and you'll find a great day together already planned out. You can read about the main event, check our age-appropriateness ratings to make sure it's right for your family, pick up some smart tips, and find out where to grab a bite nearby.

HOW TO SAVE MONEY

Taking a whole family on an outing can be pricey, but there are ways to save.

I. Always ask about discounts at ticket booths. We list admission prices only for adults and kids, but an affiliation (and your ID) may get you a break. If you want to support a specific institution, consider buying a family membership up front. Usually these pay for themselves after a couple of visits, and sometimes they come with other good perks—gift-shop and parking discounts, and so on.

2. Keep an eye peeled for coupons. They'll save you $2 or $3 a head and you can find them everywhere from the supermarket to your pediatrician's office. Combination tickets, sometimes offered by groups of attractions, cost less than if you pay each admission individually.

3. Try to go on free days. Some attractions let you in at no charge one day a month or one day a week after a certain time.

GOOD TIMING

Most attractions with kid appeal are busy when school is out. Field-trip destinations are sometimes swamped on school days, but these groups tend to leave by early afternoon, so weekdays after 2 during the school year can be an excellent time to visit museums, zoos, and aquariums. Outdoors, consider going after a rain—there's nothing like a downpour to clear away crowds. If you go on a holiday, call ahead—we list only the usual operating hours.

SAFETY CATCH

Take a few sensible precautions. Show your kids how to recognize staff or security people when you arrive. And designate a meeting time and place—some visible landmark—in case you become separated. It goes without saying that you should keep a close eye on your children at all times, especially if they are small.

FINAL THOUGHTS

We'd love to hear yours: What did you and your kids think about the places we recommend? Have you found other places we should include? Send us your ideas via e-mail (c/o editors@fodors.com, specifying the name of this book on the subject line) or snail mail (c/o Around Washington, D.C. with Kids, Fodor's Travel Publications, 201 East 50th Street, New York, NY 10022). In the meantime, have a great day around Washington with your kids!

THE EDITORS

ARLINGTON NATIONAL CEMETERY

Don't be surprised if your children click their heels together for awhile after watching the changing of the guard at the Tomb of the Unknowns. Here soldiers from the Army's 3rd U.S. Infantry Regiment (Old Guard) keep watch 24 hours a day, regardless of weather. Each sentinel marches 21 steps (children can count them silently), clicks his or her heels, and faces the tomb for 21 seconds, symbolizing the 21-gun salute—all while carrying an M-14 rifle weighing 10 pounds. Changing the guard is a precise ceremony, held every half hour during the day from April through September and every hour the rest of the year. (At night, when the cemetery's closed, it's every two hours.)

Kids may also be interested in famous grave sites. Some 260,000 American war dead and many notable Americans are interred in these 612 acres. John F. Kennedy is buried under an eternal flame near two of his children, who died in infancy, and his wife, Jacqueline Bouvier Kennedy Onassis. His is the most visited grave in the country. Nearby, marked by a simple white cross, is the resting place of his brother Robert. Famous veterans buried here include

TRANSPORTATION You can ride the Metro, take a Tourmobile bus (tel. 202/554–7950), walk across Memorial Bridge (southwest of the Lincoln Memorial), or drive. There's a large paid parking lot at the skylit visitor center on Memorial Drive. Only those with a family member buried here (and a vehicle pass) can drive within the cemetery. Others must tour on foot, which means a fair bit of hiking, but also up-close looks at the graves. To reach Ft. Myer, take U.S. 50 west to the Iwo Jima Memorial exit. Stay straight to enter the Wright Gate. MPs will provide directions to the stables.

West end of Memorial Bridge, Arlington, VA.
Metro: Arlington National Cemetery

 Free

Apr–Sept, daily 8–7; Oct–Mar, daily 8–5

703/607–8052, 703/697–2131 to locate specific grave

6 and up

Joe Louis (boxer), Lee Marvin (actor), and Abner Doubleday (reputed inventor of baseball). A memorial to the Space Shuttle *Challenger* is here as well.

While at Arlington, you will probably hear the clear, doleful sound of a bugler playing taps or the sharp reports of a gun salute. On average, 22 funerals are held here daily. You'll want to remind your child that this is sacred ground; respect and quiet are always necessary.

If you're driving and have an extra 30–60 minutes, consider taking a free tour of the stables at nearby Ft. Myer (Arlington Blvd. [U.S. 50], tel. 703/696–3147), operated by the Old Guard's Caisson Platoon and open 12–4. Your child can bring carrots or apples to feed the elegant horses (with help from soldiers), which participate in funerals at Arlington, weddings at Ft. Myer, and parades throughout D.C.

HEY, KIDS! Check out the grave of the Drummer Boy of Chickamauga (a Civil War battle). John Lincoln Clem was 9 years old when he was a drummer boy and 12 when he became an active-duty soldier—the youngest ever in the U.S. Army! He eventually retired as a major general in 1916. Clem fought for the Union, but both Union and Confederate soldiers are buried at Arlington.

KID-FRIENDLY EATS No food or drink is allowed at Arlington National Cemetery. Which side of the river you're coming from or returning to will determine where to eat. In Arlington, **Queen Bee** (3181 Wilson Blvd., tel. 703/527–3444) is one of the area's best Vietnamese restaurants; for all-American barbecue try **Red Hot & Blue** (1600 Wilson Blvd., tel. 703/276–7427). For suggestions in Washington, *see* the DAR Museum and the White House.

AUDUBON NATURALIST
SOCIETY'S WOODEND

Don't let "bad" weather keep the kids inside. In fact, no matter what it's like, there'll be something interesting to see and do at this nature sanctuary. Snow and mud make finding animal tracks easier as you play nature detective. On hot, humid days, crickets form a chorus with cicadas, and butterflies dance in wildflower meadows. On cool, crisp fall days, you can see varied leaf colors reflected in the large pond. But on any day, you'll hear the trill of birdsong, because the Audubon Naturalist Society (ANS) has turned the grounds into something of a private nature preserve, forbidding toxic chemicals and leaving some areas in their wild, natural state.

A self-guided nature trail winds through this verdant 40-acre estate and around the local ANS's suburban Maryland headquarters. The estate is known as Woodend, as is the mansion, which was designed in the 1920s by Jefferson Memorial architect John Russell Pope. Allowing time to marvel at Mother Nature, you can complete the ¾-mile trail in about 1½ hours. Parents of babies should use a backpack rather than a stroller as most of the trail has wood chips.

HEY, KIDS!
Along the nature trail, you'll not only see birdhouses and bird feeders, but also houses for flying squirrels. You can learn more about these cool creatures at an Audubon Naturalist Society flying squirrel program, held periodically throughout the year.

KID-FRIENDLY EATS Picnicking isn't allowed at Woodend without a permit, but 3 miles west, in downtown Bethesda, you can nibble your way around the world at any of 180 restaurants. **Oodles Noodles** (4907 Cordell Ave., tel. 301/986–8833) offers some of the area's best Asian cooking and best bargains. Big portions of Tex-Mex fare make **Rio Grande Cafe** (4919 Fairmont Ave., tel. 301/656–2981) a favorite for families. For a dining guide call the Bethesda Urban Partnership at 301/215–6660.

8940 Jones Mill Rd.,
Chevy Chase, MD

301/652-9188

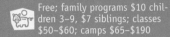 Free; family programs $10 children 3–9, $7 siblings; classes $50–$60; camps $65–$190

 Daily sunrise–sunset. Bookshop M–W and F 10–6, Th 10–8, Sa 9–5, Su 12–5

3–9

For a break from the outdoors (but not the heat—the mansion isn't air-conditioned), ask at the Woodend office if you can see the library. Along with books for adults, it contains hundreds of stuffed American birds. The mansion isn't always open to the public, however, as it's rented for weddings, bar mitzvahs, and other celebrations.

During family programs (which include parents), classes, and one- to two-week camps, educated naturalists from the society's staff foster environmental awareness and unlock nature's mysteries. Each program focuses on a nature-oriented theme, like meadow habitats, pond life, or "metamorphosis magic," and includes such hands-on activities as catching insects, fishing for pond creatures with nets, or investigating rotting log communities. ANS fairs in May and December attract thousands. While you shop at the crafts show, your children can enjoy animal demonstrations and kiddie crafts. There really is lots going on here year-round.

KEEP IN MIND Please remind your kids that you can't take it with you. Every stick, leaf, rock, and insect needs to stay at Woodend. If your little collectors are disappointed by this rule, you can visit the bookshop. It sells neat souvenirs for young naturalists, including nature books, puzzles, T-shirts, and games.

BOWIE BAYSOX BASEBALL

Minor league baseball offers major league fun for young fans of the Bowie Baysox, a Class AA Eastern League affiliate of the Baltimore Orioles. Not only can you see what's happening better at the 10,000-seat Prince Georges Stadium than at 50,000-seat major-league ballparks, but you'll find as much action off the field as there is on it.

As a Baysox player slides into base, your children can slide down the gangplank of a playground boat. (Some kids play it's a pirate ship; others pretend they're on the *Titanic*.) As players circle the diamond, your kids can circle on a carousel, which runs during the entire game, except while the national anthem plays. Little sluggers test their throwing arms in pitching games.

Meanwhile, collectors spread out baseball cards in the ample bleachers, and there's plenty of room for teenagers to move a few seats away and pretend they're not really with Mom and Dad. When the ballpark is crowded, fans get more boisterous, which is also part of the

HEY, KIDS! Do you want player autographs? It's easier to get them here than at major league stadiums. Baysox officials recommend staying a half hour after the game to catch players leaving the park. Several players move up to the majors each year, so you may get an autograph from tomorrow's star.

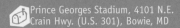
Prince Georges Stadium, 4101 N.E. Crain Hwy. (U.S. 301), Bowie, MD

301/805-6000 information, 301/805-2233 tickets

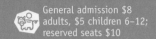
General admission $8 adults, $5 children 6-12; reserved seats $10

Early Apr–Labor Day

4 and up

entertainment. Giveaways throughout the summer can yield such precious kid keepsakes as caps, jerseys, and mugs, and children wearing youth athletic uniforms get in for free. On Saturday night and an occasional weeknight, post-game fireworks light up the sky.

Of course, if your kids are actually interested in the game itself, they can keep track of it on electronic scoreboards and a large screen that shows replays from the field and fans in the stands. (So smile! You may be on camera.) And if they come wearing their youth athletic uniforms, they'll get in free. All the activity makes minor league baseball and children a natural double-play combination. The only real downside is that your family won't see today's superstar . . . but you might see tomorrow's!

KID-FRIENDLY EATS At the **Kids' Stand,** peanut butter sandwiches, juice, and such typical baseball fare as hot dogs cost about $1 each. (Sorry, the Kids' Stand is just for kids!) Adults pay a little more at the concession stands but get more choices. You can eat pub-type fare while watching the game from the **Diamond View** restaurant, when it's open. On most weekends and some weekdays it's booked for parties.

KEEP IN MIND Two Class A minor league teams also play in Washington's outfield: the Frederick Keys (tel. 301/831-4200) in Frederick County, Maryland, and the Cannons (tel. 703/590-2311) in Prince William County, Virginia. The Bowie stadium is newer and a little larger, and since the Baysox are Class AA, the quality of play's a little better. Otherwise the experience is much the same. Based on where you live, you may want to try one of the others.

BUREAU OF ENGRAVING AND PRINTING

Show me the money! It's here—some $530 million printed daily—and any youngster who gets an allowance will enjoy watching as bills roll off the presses. Despite the lack of free samples, the self-guided 30-minute bureau tour is one of the city's most popular attractions. Video monitors and a recording provide explanations and background information on the printing process.

The United States began printing paper currency in 1862 to finance the Civil War and because there was a coin shortage. Two men and four women separated and sealed by hand $1 and $2 U.S. notes printed by private companies. Today, the bureau employs approximately 2,500 people, who work out of two buildings: this one and one in Fort Worth, Texas.

On tour, your children can look through wide windows to see three steps in the money-making process. First, both sides of the bills are printed in large 32-note sheets—back side first. (Bureau employees refer to bills as "notes.") Second, machines and employees

KID-FRIENDLY EATS A healthful meal doesn't cost much at the **U.S. Department of Agriculture cafeteria** (14th St. and Independence Ave. SW, tel. 202/488-7279). Get a visitor sticker at the front desk, and then choose from 10 food stations.

KEEP IN MIND Early April–September, required same-day timed entry passes are issued starting at 8 at the Raoul Wallenberg Place SW entrance. Waits to get in can be two hours, and if a tour bus arrives as you do, you may also wait for tickets. While waiting outside, examine some money with your kids. Once inside, video monitors with trivia questions help pass time. For example: If you spent $1 every second, it would take 317 years to spend $10 billion. A mile-high stack of currency would contain over 14½ million notes.

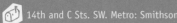 14th and C Sts. SW. Metro: Smithsonian

 Free

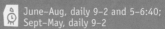 June–Aug, daily 9–2 and 5–6:40; Sept–May, daily 9–2

 6 and up

202/874–3019

inspect the notes for defects. For example, if a sheet was folded instead of flat during the process, the notes may only be half printed. Rejects are shredded and sold. In the final area, serial numbers and Federal Reserve seals are printed, and the notes are cut.

Each note costs 4¢–5.2¢ to print. Denominations of $20 and more cost a little extra because of security enhancements such as watermarks, color-shifting ink, and security threads. Hold one of these large denominations up to the light to see the vertically embedded threads. Environmentally minded kids will be glad to know that no trees are cut down to make bills; they're made of cloth: 75% cotton and 25% linen.

It may sound crazy to adults, but kids like to buy bags of shredded money in the bureau's gift shop. A small bag costing $1.50 contains $150 worth of bills that didn't pass inspection. For $5 your children can get slightly more practical mementos: postcards that look like currency with their photos on them.

HEY, KIDS! Would you like to make money? Ten-year-old Emma Brown did. She was the youngest employee in bureau history, but she didn't work here for the fun of it. Emma's brother, the family breadwinner, was killed in action during the Civil War, leaving Emma to care for her disabled mother and the rest of the family. Emma's congressman gave her a political appointment so she could make money by making money.

CAPITAL CHILDREN'S MUSEUM

Looking for a capital kid's adventure? You may find this rambling hands-on museum behind Union Station quirky, but for children it's fun, festive, and flooded with opportunities for exploration. The eclectic assortment of exhibits is about as organized as the contents of most kids' backpacks after they've been dumped on the floor. The museum was designed that way to encourage kids to go up and down and back and forth over three floors of exhibits. It works!

In the popular city room, your children can "drive" a Metro bus, whiz down a fire pole, and wander through the sewer system. Budding artists can create cartoons in the animation exhibit. In the Chemical Science Center, museum scientists mix chemistry with comedy to educate and entertain kids with zany experiments, including blowing up gummy bears, removing the iron from breakfast cereal, and electrocuting a pickle. In the center's lab, kids over 6 don lab coats and goggles to create their own slime, learn what makes diapers absorbent, or isolate vitamin C from fruit drinks.

HEY, KIDS!

Check out the third-floor bubble room. You can make a bubble large enough to hold you and a parent. When you drive the Metro bus, change the name of the stop like a real driver. For secret fun, explore the Inca pyramid in the Mexican exhibit. At the bottom, you'll discover a surprise.

KEEP IN MIND
Late afternoons (nap times) tend to be the least crowded here. Whenever you come, though, allow at least three hours for exploring this huge children's paradise. Keep an eye on your kids; there are lots of staircases and elevators, plus a maze and a cave. Also, bring a backpack or large purse to carry your children's crafts. A tissue-paper flower won't be the same after being stuck in a pocket.

 800 3rd St. NE. Metro: Union Station

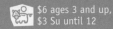 $6 ages 3 and up, $3 Su until 12

 Easter–Labor Day, daily 10–6; Labor Day–Easter, daily 10–5

 202/675-4120

1–12

Two of the larger exhibits focus on other cultures. In the Mexican exhibit, your kids can sample hot chocolate, make native crafts, climb up an Inca pyramid, and take off their shoes to enjoy a sandbox by the shore. In the Japanese exhibit, they can check out kimonos and electronics in a shopping district and pretend to be students in a Japanese classroom. Changing exhibits often feature children's literature from around the world.

In the puppet room, rocking chairs for nursing mothers and hand puppets for children make a welcome combination. Special events are held on weekends and holidays throughout the year, and story hours, theme days, and puppet shows in the large auditorium enhance the museum experience. When you've finally had enough of all those hands-on experiences, pause at the museum art gallery, near the exit, where you can unwind and simply look, for a change.

KID-FRIENDLY EATS Picnic tables can be found on the grounds and in a lunchroom with vending machines on the second floor. For heartier fare, you'll find restaurants and more than 35 food stands offering everything from pizza to sushi at **Union Station** (50 Massachusetts Ave. NE). One of the best eateries is **America** (*see* D.C. Ducks). **Johnny Rockets** (tel. 202/289-6969), a 1950s-style hamburger joint, also appeals to families.

THE CASTLE (SMITHSONIAN BUILDING)

I n London castles may be for kings and queens, but here in Washington, the Castle is for us common folk who want to map out a day on the National Mall. And since it opens an hour before the other Mall museums, early risers can get a good jump on their adventures. Called the Castle because of its magnificent towers and turrets, this first Smithsonian building is a Norman-style structure made of red sandstone. Completed in 1855, it originally housed all of the Smithsonian's operations—hard to imagine now—including the science and art collections, research laboratories, and living quarters for the institution's first secretary and his family.

Start at the Castle's Smithsonian Information Center, where you can learn all about the museum, education, and research complex—16 museums and galleries (nine of which are on the Mall) and a zoo—that is Washington's Smithsonian Institution. A 20-minute video overview plays constantly. If your kids will sit still that long, you may get to watch it. Better yet, talk to the very knowledgeable volunteers, or pick up a brochure. Touch-screen monitors at heights

HEY, KIDS! In the 1890s American buffalo (a.k.a. bison) were kept in a pen behind the Castle. These once-numerous beasts had been hunted so relentlessly for decades that their numbers were dwindling. Determined to prevent their extinction, Samuel Pierpont Langley, the Smithsonian's third secretary, convinced Congress to provide a site where bison and other animals could be protected and displayed. It was the beginning of the National Zoo. Today, around 10,000 buffalo live on protected land, but no tracks remain here.

1000 Jefferson Dr. SW. Metro: Smithsonian

 Free

 Daily 9–5:30

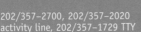 202/357–2700, 202/357–2020
activity line, 202/357–1729 TTY

2 and up

for both children and adults display information on the day's events. Interactive videos provide more detailed information on the museums as well as other attractions in the capital city. Push a button on the electronic map to locate Arlington National Cemetery or to light up the entire Metro system. A braille map of the city wasn't designed for children but draws them nonetheless.

The Castle doesn't have exhibits anymore, but some children are fascinated by the tomb of the institution's British benefactor, James Smithson, which is housed in the appropriately named Crypt Room. His bequest worth $515,169 in gold sovereigns established the Smithsonian.

On the other hand, if you're not an early riser and the day is hot, pause awhile so you can cool off by strolling through the Enid A. Haupt Garden, behind the Castle, where one of the fountains spurts water onto the path.

KEEP IN MIND
Wherever you go, here are tips to make your excursions successful: 1. When you arrive at a sight, visit the information desk for maps and brochures, and inquire about children's programs. 2. Review safety rules with your children. 3. Keep in mind that what your children want to do may be different from your own ideas for fun. 4. Take frequent breaks. 5. Try to be as spontaneous as your kids!

KID-FRIENDLY EATS
About 3 million people—more than 10% of Smithsonian museum visitors—eat at the institution's cafeterias and restaurants. The following Mall museums have eateries (*see below*): the Hirshhorn Museum and Sculpture Garden (summer only), National Air and Space Museum, National Gallery of Art, National Museum of American History, and National Museum of Natural History. The Castle opens its **dining room** (tel. 202/357–2957) to the public for Sunday brunch 11–3 and on Saturday and holidays 11–2.

C&O CANAL NATIONAL HISTORIC
PARK'S BOAT RIDES

When you hear the horn blow, boarding time is near. Your family can take a leisurely, mule-drawn barge ride through the lock, down the Chesapeake & Ohio (C&O) Canal, and back again. While you won't go far physically—less than a mile—you can travel all the way back to the 1800s in your mind while costumed guides teach about canal life. Interestingly, the Chesapeake & Ohio goes to neither the Chesapeake nor the Ohio. The B&O (Baltimore & Ohio) Railroad beat the canal to the Ohio River, and the railroad's success eventually put the canal out of business. Ironically, construction of both the C&O and B&O began on the same day, July 4, 1828. When canal construction ended in 1850, there were 74 lift-locks stretching from downtown D.C. to Cumberland, Maryland. Nevertheless, for a time the canal did prove to be economical for traders moving goods, especially coal, to the port of Georgetown, from which ships traveled to the lower Chesapeake and Atlantic Ocean.

Most children are fascinated by the canal barge's engines: Four mules named Ada, Frances, Katie, and Rhody take turns pulling the 12-foot-wide barge along the towpath. As it passes

KID-FRIENDLY EATS Drop anchor at **Washington Harbour** (3000 K St. NW, tel. 202/944–4140), a complex of condos, offices, and restaurants. Stroll the waterfront with yogurt from **TCBY** (tel. 202/298–6757), or munch popcorn shrimp from **Tony and Joe's** (tel. 202/944–4545).

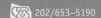 1057 Thomas Jefferson St. NW. Metro: Foggy Bottom

202/653–5190

 $7.50 ages 15 and up, $4 children 3–14

Apr–Oct, W–Su 11, 1, and 2:30 (times may change; call ahead)

3 and up

under the 15-foot-wide bridge at Thomas Jefferson Street, it may only be a canal worker's foot keeping the boat from hitting the bridge.

Don't be alarmed if your guide jumps off the boat to help with the lines and puts a child in charge for a few minutes. Said child will probably take possession of the horn and may even wear a captain's hat to make sure passengers stay in line. Eventually the guide will come back. Amid tales of canal life, he or she may treat you to some music and a few jokes. One example: "Along the canal, you may notice moss on the sides of the lock. Can you guess the name of the bird who uses the moss for its nest? The lock moss nester!" The rest of the ride should be all downhill.

HEY, KIDS! Mules, the offspring of horses and donkeys, were chosen to pull barges because of their strength and heat tolerance and because they don't require as much hay and grain as horses. To be a true mule, your mother has to be a horse and your dad a donkey. If your father's a stallion and your mom's a donkey, you're a hinny. To remember which is which, recite this simple alliteration: The mother of the mule is the mare.

KEEP IN MIND Across M Street is the oldest building in Washington: the Old Stone House (3051 M St. NW, tel. 202/426–6851), built in 1764. Here five rooms are furnished with simple, sturdy artifacts of 18th-century middle-class life but your kids might head for the garden in back, perfect for a picnic or quick game of tag. Admission is free, and the house is open Memorial Day–Labor Day, daily 8:30–4:30, and the rest of the year, Wednesday–Sunday 8:30–4:30. Teenagers might prefer Georgetown's funky boutiques.

CHILDREN'S MUSEUM OF ROSE HILL MANOR PARK

The first place kids go in this historic home is the same one they seek out in most houses: the playroom. However, the playroom of this Georgian home, the last residence of the first elected governor of Maryland, is full of replicas of toys and games from over 100 years ago: corncob checkers, a dollhouse, a cradle, a rocking horse, a tea set, a large ticktacktoe cloth, dress-up clothes, and mechanical coin banks. Lift a lever on these banks to move a penny from a whale to a boat, a monkey to a box, or Uncle Sam's arm to a little black bag.

Costumed docents meet families in the playroom, and the antique adventure continues. Upstairs there's a master bedroom, domestic quarters, a study room, and a child's bedroom with Early American toys. A 1½-hour tour at most historical sights would be too long for kids, but docents here are experienced in showing children what life was like during our country's infancy. Along the way, they explain how fireplaces, bed warmers, and windows were used in different weather. In addition, the tour includes numerous hands-on activities: Back downstairs, children can card wool, operate a loom, add stitches to a quilt, or try out

TRANSPORTATION

Rose Hill Manor is about 50 miles from D.C., but well worth the drive. Take I–270 north to U.S. 15 at Frederick. Get off at the Motter Avenue exit, and turn left on 14th Street and left on North Market Street. The entrance is just past the Governor Thomas Johnson schools.

KID-FRIENDLY EATS

Pretzels take on a new twist at **Pretzel and Pizza Creations** (210 N. Market St., tel. 301/694–9299), where the 30 varieties include chocolate, peanut butter, and rainbow sprinkle. Children's books on shelves in the back and cups of cappuccino encourage kids and their parents to linger. At **44 North Spirits & Downtown Fare** (44 N. Market St., tel. 301/698–1845), gargoyles with surprising and scary faces look down at girls and boys munching on sandwiches and ice cream sundaes.

 1611 N. Market St. (Rte. 355), Frederick, MD

  Apr–Oct, M–Sa 10–4, Su 1–4; Nov–mid-Dec, Sa 10–4, Su 1–4

 301/694–1648

 $3 adults, $2 children 3–17

4–12

18th-century cooking equipment. If the tour does get tiresome for your kids, however, you can escape to the gardens, where there's room to romp.

The tour itself continues outside to a one-room log cabin, a reminder that the majority of people in the early 1800s were not to the manor born. Most settlers lived in simple homesteads. In the blacksmith's shop, kids learn how 19th-century "smithies" spent most of their time repairing such ironwork as axes and chains. In the carriage museum, your children can find foot warmers in carriages and sleighs. Near the carriage museum, an Early American garden and orchard contains more than 100 species of herbs, flowers, fruits, and vegetables. If you're interested, the last tour stop is the requisite museum store, which carries postcards and inexpensive trinkets.

HEY, KIDS! While you're walking around Rose Hill Manor, think about the fact that houses hundreds of years ago had no closets, no bathrooms (not even running water), no electricity, no central heating, and no air-conditioning. See if you can find all the devices and solutions people employed instead of those modern conveniences.

60

Back in the 1770s, children didn't have to go to school, wear shoes, or take a nightly bath. Some modern children might even think those early days were easy—that is, until they visit this re-created Colonial farm.

Here child volunteers portraying Colonial kids (when school is closed) explain that children couldn't go to school because they worked all day on the farm. Those who could fit into one of the few pairs of shoes a family might own were lucky, as they were less likely to suffer from sore feet. Frequent baths weren't considered healthful nor were they practical, since heating enough water for a tub took a long time.

Even when the Colonial kids aren't here, you and your children can watch a pair of historical re-creators, dressed in period clothing, demonstrate how a farming couple eked out a living by tending to tobacco and wheat fields, a vegetable garden, farm animals, and family chores.

KID-FRIENDLY EATS If you packed a lunch, grab one of the picnic tables at the farm entrance. A few miles away, the **McLean Family Restaurant** (1321 Chain Bridge Rd., tel. 703/356–9883) has been serving Greek and American dishes for over 30 years. At **Rocco's Italian Restaurant** (1357 Chain Bridge Rd., tel. 703/821–3736), child-size pizzas are a best-seller, but those with more sophisticated palates can order manicotti, rigatoni, and ravioli. After eating, kids (and adults) can get a lollipop for the road.

A dirt path winds around an orchard, fields, a tobacco barn, a pond, a hog pen, and an English-style, one-room farmhouse. The walk is comfortable, and a well-napped preschooler can make the trip without wearing out. Pushing a stroller along the root-laden path is tricky, but it is possible.

During Market Fairs, held the third full weekends in May, July, and October, families enjoy making Colonial crafts (about $1 each), listening to music, and watching puppet shows. And just as in the 1770s, you can eat and shop. Check out the rosemary chicken and vegetables roasted over a fire, hot pies, and more. Reproductions of 18th-century pottery, jewelry, fragrant soaps, clothing, and toys are for sale on Market Fair days, too.

By the end of the day, your kids will probably have discovered that Colonial life was indeed tough, but you'll have discovered that a trip to Claude Moore is easy.

KEEP IN MIND
One word of warning: Encourage your kids to go to the bathroom before you arrive. The farm is equipped with the modern-day equivalent of outhouses (the portable toilet).

HEY, KIDS! When Colonial kids played, they either used their imaginations or made toys out of things that had no monetary value and weren't needed elsewhere. They made marbles out of clay and turned split sapling trees into hoops, which they rolled on the ground with a stick. Try rolling a hula hoop with a stick. It's harder than you might think, and you don't need batteries.

COLLEGE PARK AVIATION MUSEUM

W alk by the animatronic Wilbur Wright and he'll tell you about teaching pilots to fly in 1909. But children don't have to take Wilbur's word for it that learning to fly was thrilling. They'll see it for themselves at this interactive museum dedicated to early aviation.

Your children will be challenged and exhilarated as they turn and pull levers, knobs, and switches on flight simulators. They can try starting a plane's engine, not by turning a key as it's done today, but the way it was done before World War I, by turning a propeller. (Hint: Make sure no one is in the way and push down as hard as you can. Then step back. It's loud!) Your kids can even dress like pilots of yore, donning goggles, silk scarf, and helmet to pose for pictures against an airplane backdrop. (Be sure to bring a camera.) Turn on the fan to set the scarf blowing in the wind.

Also inside, a full-scale replica of the 1911 Wright B Aeroplane, a restored 1918 Curtiss Jenny, a 1932-era Monocoupe, and a Berliner Helicopter grace the largest gallery of this

TRANSPORTATION The nearest Metro stop, College Park, is a significant walk from the museum (about 15 minutes), and since it's on the Green Line, it means a transfer for many people. Driving is probably an easier way to get here, and parking is plentiful.

KID-FRIENDLY EATS If your kids just want to watch planes, bring lunch and eat on the museum balcony, overlooking the airport. At the aviation-theme **94th Air Squadron restaurant** (5240 Paint Branch Pkwy., tel. 301/699–9000), about ⅓ mile away, big-band music plays, and you can still watch the airport action, but the food is inconsistent. If you'd rather take off for guaranteed good eats, the original **Ledo's** (2420 University Blvd., tel. 301/422–8622) is about 2 miles away. Some people insist that Ledo's pizza—with cheese so gooey you need a knife and fork—is Maryland's most delicious.

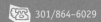
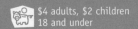

airy museum, which opened in September 1998. If you notice a similarity to the National Air and Space Museum (*see below*), you're not imagining it; both museums were designed by the same architectural firm.

Outside there's still more to see and do. Children age five and under get a feel for flying by riding around in wooden planes on a mini-runway. Gaze out the museum's large glass wall onto College Park Airport, the world's oldest continually operating airport. Referred to as the "cradle of aviation," it lays claim to the first Army aviation school, first U.S. Postal Service flight, and first female passenger to fly in the United States. But those facts probably won't interest your youngster as much as simply watching the small, single-engine planes take off and land.

KEEP IN MIND For a list of what's happening on the day you visit, check the activity board in the Experimentation Gallery. It may list Plane Talk aviation speakers, of interest to older kids, or Peter Pan Club activities, such as making paper airplanes, for preschoolers. Take home a flight of fancy from the museum's gift shop, which is full of aviation toys and games, many under $5.

CORCORAN GALLERY OF ART

Make a pop-up greeting card! Turn everyday objects into works of art! These are some of the activities in store on the four Saturdays a year designated Family Days, when one of the oldest U.S. museums offers kids workshops, demonstrations, theatrical performances, music, and tours. In addition, once or twice a month the Corcoran holds thematic tour-workshops for kids as part of its Sunday Traditions program. To celebrate those famous birthdays, for example, a February program may involve looking for portraits of presidents. Each of the Family Days and Sunday Traditions is different. Call for a calendar.

If you can't make one of these events, you can still create a fun family adventure by sharing your enthusiasm for art with your children. The permanent collection at the Corcoran, one of the few large, private museums in Washington outside the Smithsonian family, numbers more than 14,000 works, including paintings by the first great American portraitists: John Singleton Copley, Gilbert Stuart, and Rembrandt Peale. In fact, the portrait on the $1 bill was modeled on Stuart's *Portrait of George Washington*. A replica (by the artist's own hand,

KID-FRIENDLY EATS The Corcoran Gallery's **Cafe des Artistes** looks too elegant for little children, but high chairs let you know that even the littlest child is welcome. The Corcoran's Jazz Gospel Brunch on Sunday is festive for families. If you'd rather dine on paper plates than china, **Burrito Brothers** (1825 I St. NW, tel. 202/887–8266), a Mexican fast-food restaurant, is a few blocks away. For other casual eateries, *see* the DAR Museum and the White House.

not a copy by someone else) is at the gallery. Ask at the front desk if it's hanging that day; if it is, hand your kids dollar bills and have them try to find it. Photography and works by contemporary American artists are also strengths here.

If your children appreciate beauty, see the 13th-century stained-glass window that originally hung in France's Soissons Cathedral. When the sun shines, watch the colors seemingly melt onto the floor. If your kids like cartoons, check out the collection by Daumier. The exaggerated facial features in his caricatures of politicians eventually got him in trouble. (Worse than being grounded—he went to jail.) If your kids love action, show them the buffalo hunt in *Last of the Buffalo* by Albert Bierstadt. See if they can find a coyote, a prairie dog, an elk, and antelopes. It's the thrill of the hunt, after all, that makes a museum experience even more memorable.

KEEP IN MIND
Sunday Traditions are a tradition for many local families. Registration is required. You can—and many parents do—sign up six weeks in advance. In fact, it's best to call at least four weeks ahead of time or risk having the program you want be full.

HEY, KIDS! Check out the huge painting *George Washington Before York-town*, by Rembrandt Peale. One of 17 children, five of whom were named for artists, Peale took some liberties with reality. Washington's horse, Nelson, was actually brown, but Peale painted him white, perhaps to stand out against the mainly brown background. (Incidentally, at times Washington did own white horses.) After the Revolution, Nelson was retired to Mount Vernon and, in recognition of his service, was never again ridden or required to work.

DAR MUSEUM

At this museum, modern kids discover what life was like 150 years or so B.C. (before computers) as part of the Colonial Adventure program (reservations required). The journey begins with dressing the part. Boys wear decorative collars, silk vests, workmen's aprons, and three-cornered caps. Girls don calico bonnets and long skirts with white aprons, because proper Colonial ladies never showed their hair or their ankles! Docents, who are all DAR (Daughters of the American Revolution) members and who also wear Colonial garb, then lead the children on a special tour, explaining the exhibits and describing life in Colonial America. Along the way children visit the Touch of Independence exhibit, where they play with Early American toys, such as a cradle and Noah's ark, and enjoy a pretend tea party. Docents demonstrate facets of Colonial life, such as candle-making. A braille flag of the United States is also a big hit.

While the younger ones are visiting their own version of 18th century America, parents and older siblings—or anyone else who isn't the right age, here at the right time, or in

KEEP IN MIND If your children have particular interests, inform your docent. Kids with an ear for music should see the antique instruments in the Rhode Island room. You may be surprised to learn that early Americans were more likely to listen to Yankee Doodle–type tunes than Bach.

HEY, KIDS! Move over Paul Revere or, better yet, dismount! At 16, Sybil Ludington rode off on her horse to warn folks that the British had come to Danbury, Connecticut. Sybil's ride on April 25, 1777, was longer and riskier than Revere's ride two years earlier. Sybil rode sidesaddle on a big bay horse for 40 miles—26 miles more than Revere—through a dangerous no-man's land between British and American lines. A statue and painting of Sybil are in the museum.

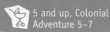

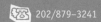

1776 D St. NW. Metro: Farragut West

202/879-3241

Free

M–F 8:30–4, Su 1–5. Tours: M–F 10–2:30, Su 1–5. Colonial Adventure usually Sept–June, 1st and 3rd Su of mth 1:30 and 3

5 and up, Colonial Adventure 5–7

the right mood for the Colonial Adventure—can take their own docent-led tour, held for small groups during the day. These tours tend to interest girls especially, as docents weave tales of women's contributions into their descriptions of many of the museum's 33 period rooms, named after states.

Besides the Touch of Independence, your kids might think the Oklahoma room, set up like a Colonial kitchen, is cool. (Try to find the toaster!) The Georgia room depicts a Savannah tavern, where citizens gathered for the state's first reading of the Declaration of Independence. In the New Hampshire room, docents describe 18th- and 19th-century dolls. And the Wisconsin room depicts a one-room house like those that only quite fortunate families could afford in Colonial times. Your children might just leave the DAR Museum not only with an understanding of Colonial life but also with an appreciation of contemporary life.

KID-FRIENDLY EATS The lines are short, but the list of selections is long at the **Bread Line** (1751 Pennsylvania Ave. NW, tel. 202/822–8900), where you can get fresh smoothies, sandwiches, and salads Monday through Friday. **Georgia Brown's** (950 15th St. NW, tel. 202/393–4499) offers down-home, yet upscale Southern-style cooking on tables covered with white butcher paper, perfect for crayon creations.

DISCOVERY CREEK CHILDREN'S MUSEUM

56

Would your children like to play dirt detectives? Romp in a swamp? Build a volcano? Watch a chameleon change colors? Discovery Creek's innovative nature programs combine outdoor adventures, art projects or experiments, and live animal demonstrations. Weekdays are primarily devoted to school groups during the school year and a camp during the summer, but on weekends the museum hosts drop-in (not drop-off) programs for families.

Located in historic Glen Echo Park (*see below*), Discovery Creek was once home to horses. Although the horses are long gone, the museum still brings the outdoors (and its creatures) in. Museum programs reflect themes that change at least twice a year. When the theme was "wetlands," 3 feet of mud was dumped on the floor, tall grass grew, and tadpoles made homes in indoor ponds. If the theme is "the desert," you'll find 3 feet of sand on the floor.

One of the smallest museums in the area, Discovery Creek provides an intimate place to learn. The scope of exploration isn't restricted, however, as every program takes advantage

HEY, KIDS!

Did you know that chocolate, chewing gum, and bananas come from plants harvested in the rain forest? Did you know that most insects can pick out four tastes, as you can: bitter, salty, sweet, and sour? At Discovery Creek, you'll do experiments and crafts that make these facts come alive.

KEEP IN MIND

Discovery Creek is a place for adventure, so dress everyone accordingly. If your children are young, you may need to provide a hand when you're climbing down the steep trail and over the creek's stepping stones. A child who is fascinated one minute could be frightened the next as a bird expands its wings or a snake uncurls. If your family enjoys the trail, come back to hike it again anytime; you don't need to attend a Discovery Creek program to enjoy it or any of Glen Echo's other treats.

of a nature trail in the woods behind the museum. Hundreds of insects scurry around a fallen tree as tall as an 11 year old, teaching about soil decomposition and animal habitats. A steep trail leads to Minnehaha Creek, where kids traverse stepping stones, searching for crayfish and other water-lovers.

Kids will be playing in the paddock where horses once did. Plans are under way to transform it into a children's botanical garden with such fun areas as a bamboo forest, tree house, and tunnel.

The museum also cares for a menagerie of animals that can't survive in the wild either because of injuries or because they were raised in captivity. Along with the wildlife and plants in the forest, these critters provide exciting, tangible activities that help kids learn about nature.

KID-FRIENDLY EATS Though you can't fish in the Minnehaha Creek, you can get fish from the **Pepperidge Farm Thrift Store** (7309 MacArthur Blvd., Bethesda, tel. 301/229–0953)—goldfish to be exact. The expiration date may be past, but you'll pay about half the retail price for crackers and cookies. Two doors down from what kids call the "fishy cracker store" are a 7-11 and a sandwich shop.

DISCOVERY THEATER

I n the midst of the mammoth museums on the Mall is a small theater that brings both our national heritage and other cultures to life. Here kids can watch what happens when Br'er Rabbit meets Coyote, learn the story of folk hero John Henry, and experience a child-size portion of Shakespeare. From popular tales to well-told, lesser-known tales from around the world, the Smithsonian's Discovery Theater lives up to its name as a place for discovery.

In the West Wing of the Arts and Industries Building, Discovery Theater is the scene of plays, puppet shows, and storytelling. Puppeteers can usually be seen manipulating their puppets in the background and sometimes even act alongside them. Young audiences are often encouraged to take part, too, by singing, clapping, or helping to develop characters and plots. And since you're never more than 10 rows away from the action at Discovery Theater, which seats up to 200 people on carpeted risers, intimacy and interaction are easy. As children react to the performers, the performers react to the children's smiles and laughter.

HEY, KIDS!
Ride a painted pony—with stripes, polka dots, even clown faces on their saddles—on a carousel in front of the Arts and Industries Building. But it's the lone dragon that attracts the most attention. Sometimes kids let others ahead of them so they're first in line for the next cycle.

KEEP IN MIND
The "Weekend" section of *The Washington Post* lists Discovery Theater performances as well as other kid-oriented shows around town. Whichever show you select (and reservations are recommended), plan to arrive 15 minutes early. If you're attending a 10 o'clock show, go around to the west entrance in the Enid A. Haupt garden, where the doors open early for Discovery Theater patrons only. Otherwise, the building itself doesn't open until 10.

Arts and Industries Building, 900 Jefferson
Dr. SW. Metro: Smithsonian

 $5 ages 1 and up

Late Sept–July, M–F 10 and 11:30, Sa
11:30 and 1

202/357–1500

2–17

Though most performances are geared to preschoolers through second graders, some are for older children and teens. Many of these performances are held in the 550-seat Baird Auditorium at the Museum of Natural History. Performances for older kids tend to be factually based presentations about historical figures or events. Past examples have included *The Meeting,* about a fictitious meeting between Malcolm X and Martin Luther King, Jr.; *From Page to Stage,* a dramatic presentation of classic and contemporary literature; and *Hades: Ride the Wild Horse,* based on mythological tales. Often productions are tied in with local schools' curricula.

Throughout the year, Discovery Theater celebrates special themes. For example, in late September and October, Hispanic heritage takes center stage, and in November, tales from Native Americans are highlighted. The most popular month for performances is February, when African-American history is celebrated with songs, stories, plays, and more.

KID-FRIENDLY EATS For a hot pretzel or an ice cream, check out the street vendors' carts in front of the building. For a complete meal, walk next door to the Hirshhorn Museum and Sculpture Garden's café (open summer only) or the National Air and Space Museum's restaurants. Across the Mall, both the National Museum of Natural History and the National Museum of American History have restaurants (*see below*).

DISCOVERY ZONE

Kids climb, jump, run, and basically go wild in their stocking feet in this indoor fitness center. Discovery Zone is loaded with tunnels, ball bins, padded cubes, and mats designed for rambunctious kids and also has a mini zone away from the main play area for babies as young as 6 months.

Surfaces are soft here. Kids fall on their faces and come up smiling. In fact, *you* are more likely to get hurt than your children, should you decide to chase them through tubes designed for micro-people. Many parents prefer to sit and watch the activity, especially those already sore from lugging around toddlers. If you plan to play with your kids in the Zone, however, leave your purse at home or use a locker. Retrieving a wallet or key chain from a bin of balls can be extremely difficult. On weekends, a crowded DZ becomes a Danger Zone. Even if your children are old enough to romp through on their own, wear socks. That way, you'll be ready to intervene if push comes to shove!

KID-FRIENDLY EATS You're not allowed to bring food to Discovery Zone, but you can purchase pizza, popcorn, and other edibles that loosely justify a place on the food pyramid. For more choices or just to get away from shrieking children—though not necessarily noisy adults—check out the popular **Cheesecake Factory** (tel. 301/770–0999) or the **food court,** both in the mall. However, there are no hand stamps for reentry; once you leave, you can't come back in unless you pay again.

If you want to shop and your kids would rather play, you can all get your way during the summer, when Discovery Zone holds two-week camp sessions for children 2–6. (While they're cavorting, you can take a leisurely excursion through the White Flint Mall.) Kids in this age range may also enjoy visiting the Zone when the Easter bunny hides eggs every spring and when Santa drops in for breakfast on two weekends before Christmas.

Older kids seeking five-second thrills may want to hang out at the arcade zone, where they can pump tokens into machines and try to win tickets that can be exchanged for trinkets. Some children become frustrated because, like all arcade games, sometimes you win, but often you lose. A return to the perpetual play area usually revives their good mood. Eventually it may be you who gets frustrated, as your child will probably want to stay here and skip his regular nap at just about the time you're ready for one.

KEEP IN MIND
While Discovery Zones across the country have been closing due to bankruptcy, including two branches in nearby Virginia, this location is independent and will continue to operate.

HEY, KIDS! Do you like arcade games? Each year many, many tickets are redeemed for goodies here. Prizes range from the two-ticket tiny and tasty—a Tootsie Roll—to the multi-hundreds-ticket huge and huggable—a stuffed animal. But don't get sucked into spending lots of money on these games. It may be tempting to keep trying to win tickets so you can get a certain prize, but remember that it would cost a *whole* lot less to just go buy that prize.

D.C. DUCKS

What do you get when you cross a tour bus with a boat? A duck, of course—that is, a D.C. Duck. Your family can tour the city by both land and water without leaving your seats aboard these unusual amphibious vehicles: standard 2½-ton GM trucks in a water-tight shell with a propeller that seat 28 intrepid passengers.

During the 1½-hour ride (reservations recommended), a wise-quacking captain entertains with anecdotes and historical trivia about Washington's memorials, monuments, and historic buildings. The captain may even quiz kids about sights along the way. Answer correctly and ding—the bell rings! For example, the captain may ask what boats are represented by the three flags near the statue of Christopher Columbus in front of Union Station. No, the answer isn't the *Love Boat,* the S.S. *Minnow,* and the *Titanic,* but rather the *Nina,* the *Pinta,* and the *Santa María.* But the part of the tour that quacks kids up the most is quacking themselves— both at tourists in town and real ducks on the water.

KID-FRIENDLY EATS Duck into **Union Station** (*see* Capital Children's Museum), a bustling train station where inaugural balls have been held. More than 35 vendors offer fast food from around the world. If you prefer a restaurant, try **America** (tel. 202/ 682–9555), whose menu of regional foods lives up to the expansive name. Kid-pleasing offerings include peanut butter with marshmallow cream sandwiches. In November and December, request gallery seating for a bird's-eye view of the station's train exhibit.

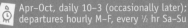
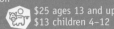

Starting along the city streets, the Duck keeps pace with traffic. Eventually it moves into the river, where it motors along at a pace only slightly faster than the feathered version for which it was named. Here kids cover their ears while watching planes take off from Ronald Reagan National Airport. As jets fly overhead, you may hear a popping sound. Little air cannons on the runways alert ducks and other birds to stay away, so they aren't killed by the engines.

While on the Potomac, your children can glimpse the Pentagon, headquarters of the Department of Defense; the Anacostia Helicopter Station, home of the presidential helicopters; and the War College, formerly Fort McNair, where the conspirators who plotted to kill Lincoln were tried, convicted, and hanged. Often children are invited to take the captain's seat and steer the Duck. When you're all done, you can add waddling through Washington and cruising around the Potomac on a Duck to your list of D.C. experiences.

HEY, KIDS! Ducks, known as DUKWs in World War II, were created to transport soldiers and supplies from ships to areas without ports. More than 21,000 DUKWs were produced, mostly by women. After the war, the Army left many DUKWs abroad, and they can still be found around the world.

KEEP IN MIND If your family is more into bikes than boats or if you'd just like to tour the city a different way, consider taking a Bike the Sites Tour (3417 Quesada St., tel. 202/966-8662). For $35 per person (including use of a bike), you can take a three-hour tour covering approximately 8 miles and 55 sights. Along the way, a guide discusses history, lore, and even scandals of the capital city. The trip is appropriate for ages 9 and older, and reservations are required 30 days in advance.

CHARLES CITY PUBLIC LIBRARY
106 Milwaukee Mall
Charles City, IA 50616-2281

EAST POTOMAC PARK

Bring your camera (everyone else does) to take a picture of your children giving high-fives to a hand more than 100 times larger than their own, sliding down a huge leg, or sitting in a monstrous mouth and living to tell about it. Or better yet, join in, and climb all over *The Awakening,* an immense statue of a man who is half buried in the ground. For some kids, he looks like a monster. Others think the bearded gent looks like dad when he's waking up. Either way, he's incredibly cool, sitting (or rather lying) at the tip of this Hains Point park, a 328-acre tongue of land that hangs down from the Tidal Basin between the Washington Channel to the east and the Potomac River to the west.

More traditional forms of recreation—tennis, golf, swimming, and miniature golf—are also available at the park and for prices that tend to be lower than at comparable enterprises.

Built during the midget golf craze of the 1920s, East Potomac Mini Golf is the oldest miniature golf course in the area. Unlike newer courses, it doesn't sport any caves, windmills, or

HEY, KIDS!

East Potomac Park is a great place to watch the planes zoom by. Every day, approximately 825 flights with about 48,450 people take off from and land at nearby Ronald Reagan National Airport.

KID-FRIENDLY EATS Pack a picnic or visit the **golf course snack bar** (tel. 202/554–7660) for a jumbo burger or sandwich. For seafood, pick a restaurant along Maine Avenue or visit its seafood market (*see* Franklin Delano Roosevelt Memorial for both). At **Captain White's Seafood City** (1100 Maine Ave. SW, tel. 202/484–2722), East Coast fish are displayed in rows. Look carefully; the stand is actually in water. The captain and his neighbors don't have seating, but you can carry out crab soup, shrimp, fish sandwiches, and more.

1100 Ohio Dr. SW, at Maine Ave.

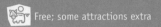 Free; some attractions extra

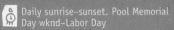 Daily sunrise–sunset. Pool Memorial Day wknd–Labor Day

202/426–6841

2 and up

fountains, but it does have native stonework and ponds with goldfish, water lilies, and a bridge. Golfers who love to do more than putter around will appreciate the challenging greens; each hole is a par-3. Kids who have moved beyond the miniature may play on two regular nine-hole golf courses, an additional 18-hole course, or just practice on the double-tier driving range or putting greens.

The long road and the parking lot make a picturesque (and perfectly flat) place to teach your child to ride a bike. The park also has outdoor tennis courts as well as courts under a bubble, which make tennis playable year-round. Reservations should be made early. A swimming pool—alas with neither diving board nor baby pool—and fishing along the Potomac (tel. 202/244–0461 for permits) round out the sporting opportunities. But be careful to visit only during the daytime; the area isn't safe after dark.

TRANSPORTATION The best way to get here is to take Ohio Drive, heading south, or Maine Avenue SW, turning off near the 14th Street Bridge, heading west, but follow signs carefully. Ohio Drive is closed to traffic from 3 PM to 6 AM on summer weekends and holidays. Going by Metro is not an option—at least not with kids. The nearest stop is a mile away.

FORD'S THEATRE NATIONAL HISTORIC SITE

The events of April 14, 1865, which shocked the nation and closed this theater, continue to fascinate both young and old. On that night, during a production of *Our American Cousin,* John Wilkes Booth entered the state box on the balcony and assassinated Abraham Lincoln. The stricken president was carried across the street to the house of tailor William Petersen, where he died the next morning.

Allow about an hour to take a self-guided tour of Ford's Theatre and the Lincoln Museum (in the basement) and to cross the street to Petersen House to see the bedroom where Lincoln died, furnished with period pieces similar to what was there then. A Junior Ranger handout, aimed at kids 6–12, sends young history detectives on a hunt to find the box where Lincoln was shot, the Derringer pistol that Booth used, and the suit that Lincoln wore that night, among other things. The book also includes activities ranging from a connect-the-dot picture of Lincoln's top hat to word scrambles. After completing the activities, each child receives a Junior Ranger badge.

HEY, KIDS! How tall are you? Probably not as tall as Abraham Lincoln, who was 6'4". But you can see just where you'd come up to on the former president by standing next to his full-size picture at the museum. Hint: You and Honest Abe side by side would make a cool photograph!

516 10th St. NW. Metro: Metro Center

 Free

 202/426-6924

 Daily 9–5. Theater closed during rehearsals and matinees (usually Th and Sa–Su); call ahead.

 6 and up

Throughout the day when the theater is open, National Park Service rangers and volunteers give 15-minute talks (some quite theatrical) about Lincoln's assassination. If you miss a presentation and your children have questions, encourage them to read the signs that accompany the displays in the museum (open even when the theater is not). Large type makes them more readable than typical museum signage. If you still have questions, talk to a ranger. It might seem strange at first to see rangers in museum settings instead of big national parks, but since Washington, D.C., is a federal district full of national monuments and historic sites, rangers are a common sight and a great resource.

KEEP IN MIND

Every year from Thanksgiving through New Year's, the ghosts of Christmases past, present, and future come to the Ford's Theatre stage in Charles Dickens's classic tale *A Christmas Carol.* (The rest of the year, performances at the theater tend to be serious adult plays.) Call 202/347–4833 for ticket information on this family favorite.

KID-FRIENDLY EATS Older kids love **Planet Hollywood** (1101 Pennsylvania Ave. NW, tel. 202/783–7827) or the **Hard Rock Cafe** (999 E St. NW, tel. 202/737–7625). The former features Hollywood memorabilia, such as Darth Vader's mask and a Klingon battle cruiser from *Star Trek;* the latter mixes rock memorabilia and tunes. For kids who haven't graduated from Raffi to rock 'n' roll or if there's a long wait, the food court at the **Old Post Office Pavilion** (1100 Pennsylvania Ave. NW, tel. 202/289–4224) may be better.

FRANKLIN DELANO ROOSEVELT MEMORIAL

If you're with toddlers, head straight to the third "room" or gallery of this memorial to our 32nd president. While children can't sit on Roosevelt's lap, they can pet Fala, Roosevelt's Scottish terrier. The tips of Fala's ears are shiny from all the attention. If you're with older children, take your time walking through the four outdoor rooms—each symbolic of one of Roosevelt's four terms. Waterfalls and reflecting pools are interspersed throughout, and children like to dangle their feet in the fountains. The granite passageways connecting the galleries are engraved with some of Roosevelt's most famous quotes, including "The only thing we have to fear is fear itself."

In the second room, challenge your children to look closely at the big bronze wall of faces, which depicts people Roosevelt put back to work after the Depression. See if you can find two men planting trees, an artist stirring paint, one farmer gathering oranges, and another driving a tractor. There's even a girl painting and a boy sculpting. Also in the second gallery, handprints along the columns, representing the working hands of the American people,

HEY, KIDS!

Fala was famous in his day. He sat at the feet of his master and British Prime Minister Winston Churchill when they signed the Atlantic Charter in 1941. The FDR gift shop is stocked with merchandise featuring the presidential pooch. A portion of all proceeds goes to the National Park Service.

KEEP IN MIND
Like many Americans in the early 20th century, at age 39 FDR contracted polio, a neural virus that left him paralyzed from the waist down. But when the memorial debuted, there wasn't much evidence of Roosevelt's disability, as there wasn't while he was president. Though he used a wheelchair, he usually kept his disability hidden from public view. However, when visiting the American war-wounded, he remained in his chair. Plans are under way to add a statue of this great president in his wheelchair.

encourage you to touch the memorial. With help from a parent, even a baby can put his hand on a print.

The fourth room has a statue of Eleanor Roosevelt. Although shy as a child, she became a vocal spokesperson for human rights.

More than recognizing Roosevelt's contributions, the memorial can help teach children about history, war, and even disability. Due to polio, Roosevelt used a wheelchair for the last 24 years of his life. A set of Roosevelt's leg braces are on display near the bookstore at the entrance of the memorial. While the FDR Memorial is a good place for children, it's even better with grandparents, many of whom lived through the Depression and World War II. And perhaps it's at its best when shared by three (or four) generations.

KID-FRIENDLY EATS For refreshments, *see* the Lincoln Memorial. A short drive away, **Maine Avenue Seafood Market** (1100 Maine Ave. SW) carries fresh fish and shellfish. Seven restaurants along Maine Avenue include local seafood powerhouse **Phillips Flagship** (900 Water St. SW, tel. 202/488–8515). All have terraces overlooking the Washington Channel and the boats moored there.

FREDERICK DOUGLASS NATIONAL

HISTORIC SITE

Most tours of historic mansions dwell on how the wealthy lived—their fancy four-poster beds, oil paintings, mahogany furniture, and beautiful china. Your children can see those things at Cedar Hill, Frederick Douglass's last home, but the main focus is on this remarkable man, who paved a path to freedom and equality for all people.

The 75-minute tours (reservations recommended) begin on the hour (except noon) in the visitor center, where a wall is devoted to the prolific speaker and writer's quotations. Among the more famous ones is, "I would unite with anybody to do right and with nobody to do wrong." Here your children can shake hands with the bronze statue of Douglass, shiny gold from all that shaking. The visitor center also has family photographs and a gift shop with books about Douglass.

Next you can watch *Fighter for Freedom: The Frederick Douglas Story*. Douglass knew neither his mother, a slave, nor the identity of his father, a white man. At age 8, he was sold to a

HEY, KIDS! Check out the portraits here. Many of the people represented were abolitionists (people who worked to end slavery), suffragists (people who sought to give women the right to vote), or, like Douglass, both. Look for Susan B. Anthony, John Brown, Elizabeth Cady Stanton, and Harriet Tubman. You can also search for a checkerboard, music box, invalid chair, and dumbbells. What you won't find are Douglass's books—more than 1,200 of them—because they're stored in a temperature-controlled environment to last for future generations to study.

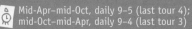

man in Baltimore, where he was exposed to the "mystery of reading" and decided that education was "the pathway to freedom." At 20 he escaped and became an abolitionist, women's rights activist, author, editor of an antislavery newspaper, minister to Haiti, and the most respected 19th-century African-American orator.

After the film, follow a park ranger to Cedar Hill, the first designated Black National Historic Site. Rangers focus on Douglass's life when in the house, first with Anna Murray, his wife of 40 years, and after her death, with second wife Helen Pitts, who was not only 20 years his junior but also white. He simply explained that his first wife was the color of his mother, his second the color of his father. While the tour is best for children who have studied American history, rangers are skilled at engaging kids as young as kindergartners. Children learn not only about the past but also about the importance of freedom and equality, even today.

KID-FRIENDLY EATS Unfortunately, you can't eat lunch on the porch of Cedar Hill. The only place to eat on site is on the grassy hill near the visitor center, next to the parking lot. There aren't any picnic tables, however, so you might want to have your meal before or after you arrive. *See* East Potomac Park for some suggested eateries.

KEEP IN MIND To enhance your children's appreciation of Cedar Hill, talk about Frederick Douglass, the Civil War, and the Civil Rights movement before you arrive. Though *Fighter for Freedom: The Frederick Douglas Story* is enlightening, this 17-minute film depicts a graphic beating he got when he was a slave. Some children and even adults find it disturbing, not just because of the violence but because it confronts a shameful part of our history. Encourage your kids to talk about their feelings and ask questions.

GLEN ECHO PARK

Years ago, Washingtonians took the trolley to Glen Echo's amusement park. Though neither the amusement park nor the trolley survive (and the closest Metro isn't close), Glen Echo, on the D.C. border, is still a magnificent and easily accessible park. It offers kids almost as many choices of activities as the historic Dentzel Carousel, in the park's center, offers choices of mounts, which range from a painted pony and a majestic lion to a saber-toothed tiger and an ostrich.

The arts thrive here. The 192-seat Adventure Theater stages such children's productions as *Charlotte's Web, Robin Hood,* and *Aesop's Fables* weekends year-round. Children sprawl on carpeted steps along with their families. At the Puppet Co. Playhouse, skilled puppeteers manipulate a variety of puppets in classic plays and stories. *Circus,* in the spring, and *Nutcracker,* in winter, are among the most popular productions. After performances, puppeteers often greet children, show how the puppets move, and answer questions about their craft. Reservations are recommended for this popular puppet place.

HEY, KIDS! Recycling is hardly a new concept. Just step into the Clara Barton House for a taste of how people recycled a century ago. Newspapers weren't put out in bins to be collected in front of your house; they were put into the house as insulation. Old sheets weren't cut up for Halloween costumes; they were ripped to make bandages for the war wounded. And 19th-century recyclers didn't have to worry about plastic soda bottles; they hadn't been invented yet.

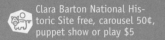

 7300 MacArthur Blvd., at Goldsboro Rd., Glen Echo, MD

301/492-6282

 Clara Barton National Historic Site free, carousel 50¢, puppet show or play $5

 Daily 9–5. Historic site tours daily 10–4. Puppet shows W–Su. Plays Sa–Su

2–16, plays 4–12

Nature holds its own at Glen Echo Park. In the former stables, a second Discovery Creek Children's Museum (*see above*) offers nature programs with live animal demonstrations, crafts, and outdoor adventures. A local Eagle Scout candidate established nature trails around Minnehaha Creek for the museum.

History has its place, too, and children who have studied the Civil War or women's history may enjoy a tour of the Clara Barton National Historic Site. Known as the "angel of the battlefield" for nursing wounded soldiers, Clara Barton founded the American Red Cross. National Park Service rangers conduct 35-minute tours that give insight into her life and Glen Echo at the turn of the last century.

Last, but certainly not least, the park is also a great spot for recreation. When your kids need to let off steam, there's plenty of space to run around and a playground with a teeter-totter that can accommodate a dozen children.

KID-FRIENDLY EATS When the carousel at Glen Echo is open (April–October on most Wednesdays and Thursdays 10–3 and most weekends 11–6:30), so is the adjacent **snack bar.** But whether you bring or purchase food, you'll find enough picnic tables and wide open spaces here to accommodate dozens of families.

GODDARD SPACE FLIGHT CENTER

Not nearly as glitzy, large, or crowded as the Smithsonian's Air and Space Museum, this NASA-run museum, called the Visitor Center, brings space flight down to earth while letting imaginations soar. Though the center wasn't designed specifically for children, even toddlers are amused by the many buttons and earphones that accompany the exhibits.

Among the real spacecraft on display is the compact car–size *Gemini XII* capsule, where astronauts Buzz Aldrin and Jim Lovell spent four days. But it's the replica of the *Gemini XII* that really excites youngsters, because they can go inside and play with 100 buttons and knobs (count them!). Press a black button and you hear the famous countdown to takeoff.

After a trip aboard the *Gemini,* kids may want to design their own satellites and rocket systems at computer stations. The computers provide all sorts of information about building rockets and will even alert you if you're over budget. (Those not as directly interested in space might prefer the Earth Science Gallery, where interactive computer kiosks explore climate

TRANS-PORTA-TION From the Baltimore-Washington Parkway (I–295) or Capital Beltway, exit to Route 193 east (Greenbelt Road). Pass the Goddard Space Flight Center, continue ¾ mile to Soil Conservation Road, and turn left. Take the next left on Explorer Road, and follow signs.

KEEP IN MIND Would your child enjoy building a terrarium, creating a glow-in-the-dark constellation, or learning the basics of rocketry? On the second and fourth Sundays of each month from 2 to 4, Goddard goes overboard with creative programs geared for different ages. Sign up at the visitor center. You don't need to sign up for Goddard's one-hour tours, which take you behind the scenes to the Hubble Space Telescope Operations Control Center and NASCOM, where NASA communicates with space shuttles and satellites. Also watch for such special events as model rocket launches and space videos.

 Building 88, Explorer Rd., Greenbelt, MD

 Free

Daily 9–4. Tours Jan–Apr, M–F 11:30, Su 11; May–Dec, M–F 11:30 and 2:30, Su 11; some Su also 2

301/286-8981;
301/286-8103 TDD

2 and up, tours 8 and up

and weather.) For children who aren't ready for computerized rocket science or for those who want to design in full color, a table is set up with paper and crayons under a sign that says, WHAT CAN YOU DRAW? THE UNIVERSE IS THE LIMIT. Kids can then trade in their finished drawings at the information desk for lithographs of rockets and space shuttles.

Information desk volunteers are also happy to try to answer children's questions, no matter how complex or off-the-wall. For example: What kind of fuel do rockets use? Usually it's kerosene or liquid hydrogen combined with liquid oxygen in a combustion chamber. Are there really space aliens? NASA's research has not confirmed that!

Outside the center is a "rocket garden," with a real 92-foot Delta rocket and other authentic space hardware. You can also see other buildings at this sprawling government complex where scientists and engineers monitor spaceships circling the earth, the solar system, and beyond.

KID-FRIENDLY EATS If you're wondering what astronauts eat, check out the fast food for space flight on display here. Then for a taste of the real thing, purchase astronaut's freeze-dried ice-cream sandwiches in foil pouches at the gift shop. The ice cream sounds more exciting than it is; it's messy and not particularly tasty. Picnicking is permitted on the grounds, but the only food sold at the facility is from a vending machine. Several fast-food restaurants are on Route 193 in Greenbelt.

HIRSHHORN MUSEUM AND
SCULPTURE GARDEN

46

Any child who thinks art museums only display boring two-dimensional paintings of old-fashioned people is in for a surprise at the Hirshhorn. Here a brightly colored fish mobile made of metal and glass swims. A wet dog in bronze walks. Life-size people made of plaster ride a bus.

American artists such as Eakins, O'Keeffe, Pollack, Rothko, and Stella are represented along with modern European and Latin masters, including Fernando Botero and Juan Muñoz, Magritte and Miró. The Hirshhorn's impressive collection includes one of the largest public collections of works by Henry Moore in the United States, as well as works by Willem de Kooning and others.

Okay, so most kids won't recognize or particularly care about these names. To make your museum experience fun for the inexperienced museum-goer, visit the information desk for a free "Family Guide." It's full of colorful art cards that encourage your children to search

HEY, KIDS!
Some kids think artists only use paint and canvases. Here at the Hirshhorn, art is made from mud, twigs, leaves, stone, light, video monitors, and even fat. Go to the plaza and find Kenneth Snelson's *Needle Tower.* Get in the center of this tall sculpture and look up. You'll see a star!

KEEP IN MIND The Hirshhorn suggests that you connect artworks with experiences meaningful to your child. When you view George Segal's *Bus Riders,* on the third floor, you could discuss where the riders might be going. Picasso's *Woman with a Baby Carriage,* also on the third floor, might elicit a story about pushing your own baby in a carriage. Although children are encouraged to get to know the art, please remind your kids not to get too friendly. The artwork is for the eyes, not the fingers.

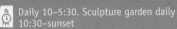

for a work, learn something about it, think about it, and relate it to their own lives and imagination. For example, on the card about Claes Oldenberg's *Geometric Mouse: Variation 1, Scale A,* kids are challenged to wonder what it would be like to be a geometric mouse visiting a mouse house with 500 other geometric mice. To design a tour for your family, allow your kids to choose their own art cards and go to the youngest child's selections first.

Two Saturday programs are especially attractive to youngsters. Young at Art allows early grade schoolers (accompanied by an adult) to tour select exhibits and create their own contemporary art using some of the techniques or materials they've seen. Saturday matinees feature family-oriented movies—short films and documentaries—unlike anything aired on the Cartoon Network. Recent flicks have included those about teeth and the environment. Both Saturday programs are offered sporadically and require reservations, so calling ahead is a must.

KID-FRIENDLY EATS For sandwiches, salads, and sculpture, the museum's outdoor café, **Full Circle,** is open Memorial Day through Labor Day from 11:30 to 3. Regrettably they don't serve the Hirshhorn's nickname, the Doughnut on the Mall, coined by detractors who didn't like the cylindrical architecture of the museum when it opened in 1974. But they do serve round personal-size pizzas.

IMAGINE THAT! DISCOVERY MUSEUM

P art playroom, part museum, Imagine That! has 35 activity areas for children to explore. One minute your child can be a painter, the next moment a pianist, a newscaster, or a doctor.

Aspiring dancers have two options. In the traditional studio, children dress up in tutus and ballet or tap shoes and let their feet fly. In the shadow room, dance fever is the rule as kids push a button that gives them about 20 seconds to pose against a light-sensitive screen. Then a light flashes, and the kids can look at their shadows and repeat the process. And they do—over and over.

Transportation-loving tots can hop a real fire truck, a wooden jeep, and a Cessna six-seater airplane complete with control tower. In the three-level wooden pirate ship, youngsters walk the plank or slide and play down below in the galley that they call "the dungeon." Just as in real life, the grocery store is often crowded, as children take turns shopping and ringing

KEEP IN MIND To save money, you have a few options. If you think you'll return again and again, buy a super-value book ($60), containing 10 kid's admission tickets and café coupons, or become members ($75), providing a year of half-price child's admission and free entry for you. If you just want to go twice in one day (with a little shopping, lunch, or nap in between), get everyone's hands stamped before you leave. To spend money, stop by Buy Buy Baby (Congressional Plaza, tel. 301/984–1122) for everything from baby basics—diapers, wipes, and clothes—to furniture for infants to preschoolers.

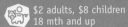
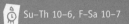

up purchases. In one of the more active areas, kids hurl beanbags with Velcro strips onto carpeted walls to play ticktacktoe or just to show their strength.

Several areas are equipped with telephones, so children can talk to their peers in other spaces. And while your kids keep track of new friends, you can keep track of your kids. Most areas are divided by low partitions that adults can peer over, and there's only one exit.

This Imagine That! was started by local mom Joyce Schneider, who observed how much her own children enjoyed the original Imagine That! in New Jersey. Since the Rockville location has 16,000 square feet of fun, your kids will probably want to stay far longer than you do!

HEY, KIDS! Send a coin spinning down a spiral wishing well in the café and do a good deed. Each month, Imagine That! donates all the money to a different children's charity. You can find out more about the charity by looking at the café's bulletin board.

KID-FRIENDLY EATS No outside food is allowed. The on-site **café** features such kid-friendly fare as pizza and hot dogs, plus a few healthful items like yogurt and carrot sticks. Behind Imagine That!, in Congressional Plaza, are two popular chains: **Starbucks** (tel. 301/230-2079), for coffee and sandwiches, and **Baskin Robbins** (tel. 301/881-3831), for ice cream. Tables outside this strip mall offer great opportunities to people-watch.

JEFFERSON MEMORIAL

Many children and adults may be surprised to learn that Thomas Jefferson didn't list being president as one of his greatest accomplishments. When he appraised his own life, Jefferson wanted to be remembered as "Author of the Declaration of American Independence, of the Statute of Virginia for religious freedom, and Father of the University of Virginia."

The monument honoring the third president is the southernmost of the District's major monuments, four long blocks and a trip around the Tidal Basin from the Metro. Jefferson had always admired the Pantheon in Rome (the rotundas he designed for the University of Virginia and his own Monticello were inspired by its dome), so architect John Russell Pope drew from the same source when he designed this memorial. But even children who have never heard of Rome, not to mention Jefferson, can still enjoy one of the city's best views of the White House from the memorial's top steps.

KID-FRIENDLY EATS A short drive away in East Potomac Park (*see above*) is a golf course snack bar with more reasonable prices than most Mall vendors, as well as the awesome *Awakening* sculpture.

KEEP IN MIND Every spring, Washington eagerly waits for the delicate flowers of the cherry trees to bloom (many of which are near the memorial). Park Service experts try their best to predict when the buds will pop—usually for about 10–12 days at the beginning of April. But regardless of when they flower, the weeklong National Cherry Blossom Festival (tel. 202/547–1500 for dates and information) is celebrated with the lighting of a ceremonial Japanese lantern, fashion shows, and a parade. When the weather complies and the blossoms are at their peak for the festival, Washington rejoices.

Inside the monument a 19-foot bronze statue of Jefferson on a 6-foot granite pedestal looms larger than life. And just in case your children didn't take the National Park Service ranger recommendation to research Jefferson before visiting the monument, they can learn about this Renaissance man by reading his writings about freedom and government on marble walls surrounding the statue. The whole family can take advantage of ranger programs offered throughout the day or ask questions of the ranger on duty.

In 1999, an exhibit called Life and Liberty was added on the lower level. It provides highlights of Jefferson's life, a time line of world history during his lifetime, an etched-glass sculpture with Jefferson's words in his own handwriting, and a 10-minute video. When you've seen it all, you and your child can judge for yourselves what Jefferson's greatest accomplishments really were.

HEY, KIDS! Built during World War II, the Jefferson Memorial sparked controversy due to its cost: a then–whopping $3,192,312. Actually, the first statue erected was made of plaster, because bronze was too expensive and was needed for the war. The bronze statue you see today was not put in place until 1947.

J. EDGAR HOOVER FBI BUILDING

Kids have played good guys and bad guys for centuries. The one-hour FBI (Federal Bureau of Investigation) tour gives children a behind-the-scenes look at how real-life, modern good guys and gals catch criminals. After a brief video outlining the bureau's work, the tour takes in exhibits that cover both famous cases and the methods the FBI uses to fight organized crime, terrorism, bank robbery, espionage, extortion, and other nefarious activities.

You'll see everything from gangster John Dillinger's death mask and a poster display of the bureau's 10 Most Wanted to laboratories where the FBI studies evidence. Of particular interest in an exhibit of 5,000 guns and ammunition are some weapons concealed in ordinary-looking objects, including a combination walking cane/shotgun that was available by mail order for $5 in the early 1900s.

Guides answer kids' questions throughout. Often children ask if X-files are kept here and if there's a jail in the building. Of course, the answer to both questions is no. But some truths

KEEP IN MIND If you have extra time, travel up to the observation deck in the clock tower at the Old Post Office (1100 Pennsylvania Ave., at 12th St., NW, tel. 202/606-8691). Although not as tall as the Washington Monument, it offers as impressive a view. Even better, it's usually not as crowded, the windows are bigger, and—unlike the monument's windows—they're open, allowing cool breezes to waft through. A tour of the tower (open mid-April–Labor Day, daily 8 AM–10:45 PM and September–March, daily 10–5:45) takes about 15 minutes.

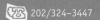 10th St. and Pennsylvania Ave. NW (tour entrance: 9th and E Sts.). Metro: Gallery Place, Archives, Federal Triangle, and Metro Center

   Tours M–F 8:45–4:15

202/324-3447

Free

7 and up

are stranger than fiction. One of the bureau's most wanted fugitives was apprehended in 1967 after a couple who were taking a tour on their honeymoon recognized his photograph.

The high point of the tour is also the part that some parents feel glorifies guns. A special agent demonstrates three weapons behind glass in the building's indoor shooting range. The agent then discusses what kids should do if they ever see a weapon. Other children's safety issues—at play and using the Internet—are covered in a video.

At peak times, there may be a 2½-hour wait for a tour. The first-come, first-served line starts to form at 7:30 AM—that's over an hour early, folks. Your only other option is to write your congressperson for passes up to three months ahead of time. Either way, many people feel it's worth the wait.

KID-FRIENDLY EATS For familiar fare, head across the street to **Mc-Donald's** (911 E St. NW, tel. 202/347–1488) or **Wendy's** (913 E St. NW, tel. 202/639–9364). Or try any of the restaurants in the airy central courtyard of the **Old Post Office Pavilion** (*see* Ford's Theatre National Historic Site).

HEY, KIDS! If taking the tour makes you curious about becoming an agent, there are a few things you should know. To become an agent, you must be a college graduate between the ages of 23 and 37 and in excellent health. You must undergo extensive background checks and then go through 16 weeks of rigorous training in Quantico, Virginia. There are between 11,000 and 12,000 agents today, and women couldn't become agents until 1972.

KENILWORTH NATIONAL
AQUATIC GARDENS

Children like to run through this 12-acre national park devoted to aquatic plants. However, the best way to enjoy this sanctuary is to walk quietly and pause often, hearing bullfrogs croak and birds chirp, searching for turtles and frogs among platter-size leaves, and gazing upon exotic plants and water lilies reminiscent of a Monet painting.

Intersecting trails surround dozens of ponds filled with plants that awe and amuse, like the extraordinary South American *Victoria amazonica,* with leaves as large as a sixth grader. Ask your youngsters how cattails and yellow flag irises got their names or whether pickerelweeds and rose mallow shrubs (no relation to marshmallows) look as silly as they sound. Watch for frogs jumping onto lily pads, turtles sunbathing, and crayfish burrowing mud chimneys to escape from turtles and birds. You might see blue herons, bald eagles, and muskrats near the river, but don't restrict yourselves to sight and sound. Let your other senses, like touch and smell (tasting isn't recommended), help you explore the park, too.

HEY, KIDS!

Did you know frogs hibernate, living under the mud? (So please don't throw pebbles in the pond.) Did you know some people think early settlers pulled used cones from the buttonbush to make buttons? Did you know water boatman bugs swim upside down on the ponds in summer?

KEEP IN MIND

Driving directions are tricky; it's best to call ahead. If you do get lost, you should know that locals refer to Kenilworth as "lily ponds." Keep a careful eye on children, especially preschoolers, while they search for aquatic life. Although the ponds are only 3 feet deep, the banks can be slick and there are no fences around them. The only barriers are those in the ponds, designed to protect the plants. You are what protects your kids, but don't worry if their clothes get a little dirty. It's all part of the fun.

The best time to visit is 8–11, when day-bloomers are opening and night-bloomers have yet to close. Water lilies flower through the summer. Pick up maps at a tiny visitor center: one for the ponds and one for the Anacostia River trail, at whose end you can see beaver hutches at low tide. Incidentally, unlike the beavers who gnawed down cherry trees on the Mall in 1999, the Kenilworth beavers are helpful. By dining on water lilies, they keep the plants from getting too crowded to flower.

If you have young children, ask for a treasure list, which changes every few months. In winter, you can search for the shells of pond crustaceans left by birds and follow animal tracks. Do you think the bird got away, or did the fox eat last night? In spring, you may hunt for muskrat holes in the dikes or watch female dragonflies dip their tails in the water to lay eggs. Whatever the season, it's fun watching kids explore Kenilworth.

KID-FRIENDLY EATS There aren't any restaurants within walking distance of these gardens tucked away in a corner of Northeast Washington, and the only food or drink available here is a water fountain at the visitor center. Instead, pack a lunch and take advantage of the picnic tables near the ponds.

KENNEDY CENTER FOR THE
PERFORMING ARTS

41

The Kennedy Center looks like a place for adults in tuxedos and black dresses, and it is. But it's also a place that rolls out the red carpet for children. As the nation's performing arts center, it takes seriously its responsibility to make an eclectic calendar of top-notch performances accessible to many. One example is the dark red Show Shuttle, which runs between the center and Foggy Bottom every 15 minutes.

More than 100 family events are held each year through Imagination Celebration (late September–early May), in which actors, dancers, storytellers, musicians, and puppeteers show off for kids. The National Symphony Orchestra puts on Kinderkoncerts. Arrive 45 minutes early, and your children can beat drums, blow into a tuba, or clang cymbals.

As part of the Performing Arts for Everyone Initiative, free one-hour performances are held nightly at 6 on the Millennium Stage (neither ticket nor reservation required). Many provide the perfect opportunity to introduce children to classical music or opera. In others, dancers,

KEEP IN MIND Cue sheets for many children's performances are available on the Kennedy Center's Web site (Kennedy-center.org). Not only do the cue sheets provide background information on the performers and their art, but they often give kids a list of things to look for when watching a show. If you can't catch Millennium Stage performances at the center, you can see them live every evening on the center's web site or on the east front lawn of the Capitol at noon on Tuesday and Thursday, early June–late August. Check *The Washington Post* for listings of children's events.

2700 F St. NW. (New Hampshire Ave. and Rock Creek Pkwy. NW). Metro: Foggy Bottom

202/467–4600 or 800/444–1342

Free, children's performances free–$10

Daily 10–9 (or until last show lets out). Box office M–Sa 10–9, Su 12–9

3 and up

actors, storytellers, or magicians reach out to kids of all ages. Performers have included Frank Sinatra, Jr., and the Duke Ellington Orchestra, as well as local artists. Seats are generally plentiful, though kids often sit up front or on the steps, or they don't sit at all—they dance! Sometimes performers sign autographs and pose for photos. During the September open house, at least one stage is devoted to children's performances, and face painters and clowns roam the halls.

Even without seeing a performance, however, you can enjoy this six-theater memorial to President Kennedy. Pick up a "flag sheet" at the information desk, and visit the Hall of Nations and Hall of States, where the flags of more than 140 countries and all 50 states hang, the latter in order of admission to the union. Take a break on the terrace overlooking the Potomac, and watch airplanes above, boats below, and the Watergate building, Jefferson Memorial, Washington Monument, and Georgetown University before you.

HEY, KIDS! The 618-foot-long Grand Foyer is one of the world's largest rooms. If you could lay the Washington Monument on its side in the Grand Foyer, you would still have about 3 inches to spare. Look up, and you'll see tons of crystal—literally. Each of the 18 chandeliers weighs one ton.

KID-FRIENDLY EATS For restaurants with a view, you can't beat the top of the Kennedy Center. The **Encore Cafe** offers self-serve soup, sandwiches, pasta salads, and pizza overlooking the Potomac and Georgetown. The formal **Roof Terrace Restaurant** isn't appropriate for most kids, but the adjacent **Hors d'Oeuvrerie** (reservations recommended) should be fine. The cheese and fresh fruit plate is huge, and desserts are big enough to split. Service is quick at all these restaurants, ensuring that you get to the show on time!

KIDSHOP

Kids don't have to sing "If I Had a Hammer" at this wood workshop just for them; they have one—and plenty of other real tools, too. KidShop staff members guide would-be carpenters through every step in the woodworking process from safety to sawing. No experience is necessary, and all classes include materials and safety goggles. The end result, which can take from a few hours to a week to complete, is a kid-built birdhouse, marble maze, treasure box, or other creation.

For those children too young to work without an adult (ages 4–6), there's Wood Play, a 1½-hour introduction to woodworking. Working as a team, you and your child—wearing goggles and gloves—assemble a simple project, such as a wood person or small memo pad holder. Older children work independently to complete more challenging projects in two-hour classes. More ambitious projects, such as making bookshelves or treasure trunks, are completed during mini-camps: weeklong, 1½- to 3-hour classes. Birthday boys and girls can "let the wood times roll" at this popular party spot, selecting a special project for their guests to complete.

KID-FRIENDLY EATS Two blocks away, **Mark's Kitchen** (7006 Carroll Ave., Takoma Park, tel. 301/270–1884) specializes in vegetarian and Asian food but also serves hot dogs. When only pizza will do, **Taliano's** (7001 Carroll Ave., Takoma Park, tel. 301/270–5515) is the place to go.

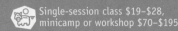

But in all workshops, everyone in the group makes the same item. Some projects require precision, like measuring and cutting accurately so the lid of a box fits. Others, such as rocket-building, focus more on creativity, as kids choose to position wings and engines differently. When your kids get home, they can add more special touches by painting, stenciling, and varnishing their creations.

Class sizes are limited and weekends are the most popular, so calling ahead is a must. Before Mother's Day, Father's Day, and other holidays, gift-making is in full swing as kids hammer out paper and pen holders, breadboards, and mini-easels for displaying their photographs and artwork. But KidShop is about more than building projects; it's about building confidence.

TRANSPORTA-TION KidShop is located off Carroll Avenue, adjacent to Takoma Park, Maryland, and is five minutes from Metro's Takoma station. It is accessible from the Beltway via the Georgia Avenue exit and from neighboring areas via the East-West Highway or 13th Street NW.

KEEP IN MIND If you have a child old enough to work with wood and another who likes to play on wood, you can take the little one to a nearby playground with wooden equipment and toddler swings at the corner of Carroll Avenue and Westmoreland Street. Teens might be more interested in nearby Takoma Park's funky shops, which carry jewelry and beads but not much wood. Ask for a town map at KidShop.

LINCOLN MEMORIAL

Give your kids five, as in five dollars. Or give them a penny. Either way, they'll see a picture of the Lincoln Memorial. Then take them to the real thing. Many consider the Lincoln Memorial the most inspiring monument in the city, and it's also one of the most kid-friendly.

Children eager to show off newly acquired counting skills will find plenty to keep them busy here. Thirty-six Doric columns, representing the 36 states in the country at the time of Lincoln's death, surround the somber statue of the seated Lincoln. Above the frieze are the names of the 48 states of the union when the memorial was dedicated in 1922. (Alaska and Hawaii are noted by an inscription on the terrace leading up to the memorial.)

Older children may practice their oratorical skills by reciting two of Lincoln's great speeches—the Second Inaugural Address and the Gettysburg Address—which are carved on the north and south walls. In addition, the Lincoln Memorial has served as a backdrop for other famous speeches, including Martin Luther King's "I Have a Dream" speech in 1963.

KID-FRIENDLY EATS A **refreshment stand** (French Dr., on north side of Independence Ave. SW) serves sandwiches, fries, chicken fingers, and so on, just a short walk from the memorial.

KEEP IN MIND If your children are intrigued by what they find at the memorial and would like to learn more about Lincoln, take them to the Ford's Theatre National Historic Site (*see above*), another site run by the National Park Service.

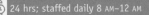
  West end of Mall NW. Metro: Foggy Bottom

 202/426-6841

Free

24 hrs; staffed daily 8 AM–12 AM

3 and up

Though many visitors look only at the front and interior of the monument, there is much more to explore. On the lower level to the left of the main stairs is Lincoln's Legacy, a display that chronicles the memorial's construction. A video and photos depict famous demonstrations and speeches that have taken place here, and another exhibit shows postage stamps from around the world that feature Lincoln on them.

If you don't need to get home for an 8:30 bedtime, come at night, one of the best times to see the memorial. (Though minimal parking is available along Ohio Drive during the day, additional parking is available in the evening along Constitution Avenue.) Spotlights illuminate the exterior, whereas inside, light and shadows play across Lincoln's gentle face.

HEY, KIDS! The statue of Lincoln is actually composed of 28 separate pieces of marble, which were hand-carved individually and then only assembled when they arrived at the memorial chamber. The face and hands look especially lifelike because they are based on castings done of Lincoln while he was president. You might find it hard to take your eyes off them.

MADE BY YOU

As the explosion of craft kits on the market can attest, kids love creating their own masterpieces and take more pride and satisfaction in making their own souvenirs and gifts than in going out and buying them (even with your money). Made By You, a paint-your-own-pottery studio, does craft kits one better.

Children choose from over 150 items to paint, including ceramic mugs, piggy banks, animal boxes, dinosaurs, picture frames, and, of course, tiles. After the paint dries, the ceramic pieces are fired in a kiln, and the result is a professional-looking product that's ready to be picked up in four days. For children who won't be around in four days or who just want instant gratification, the studio carries glass and terra cotta items, which can be painted and taken home the same day. Popular glass items include bowls, plates, and glasses, and, you guessed it, flowerpots are the number one terra-cotta treasure.

For those who want to do more than "just" paint, workshops are held at least once a

HEY, KIDS!
Cleveland Park's dogs and cats can count on a cool drink of water from the ceramic doggie and kitty bowls that sit in front of Made By You. So it should come as no surprise that ceramic pet bowls are a popular item for young artistic animal lovers to make at the store.

KEEP IN MIND Made By You is a challenging place to take an inquisitive toddler. There's plenty of easily accessible and easily broken items for little fingers to get into. On the other hand, many parents bring in their infants to put hand or footprints on plates. If this location isn't convenient for you, there are two others in the area: in Bethesda, Maryland (4923 Elm St., tel. 301/654–3206), and Arlington, Virginia (2319 Wilson Blvd., tel. 703/841–3533).

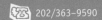
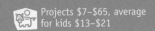

3413 Connecticut Ave. NW. Metro: Cleveland Park

202/363–9590

Projects $7–$65, average for kids $13–$21

M–Sa 10–9, Su 11–6

4 and up

month. At these, adults and kids engage in lots of clay play that may include creating picture frames, making mosaics, or rolling, cutting, and painting beads.

Gather a group of six or more children, and you can arrange for your own gala here. With three weeks advance notice, the staff will help you plan a two-hour pottery-painting party for your birthday child or scout troop. Made by You will also help with fund-raising projects. A picnic table with tiles decorated by children brought in $1,000 for one local school.

But one of the best things about craft-making at Made By You never leaves the store. Though it might get to be a bad habit if they could get away with it every day, your children won't have to clean up after themselves—but then neither will you. That dreaded chore is left to the staff of Made By You. That alone, not to mention the smile on your children's faces, can be worth the slightly pricey cost of these semi-handmade creations.

KID-FRIENDLY EATS If after that special craft goody has been made by you and your child, you feel like an edible goody made by someone else, visit the **Firehook Bakery** (3411 Connecticut Ave. NW, tel. 202/362–BAKE). The specialties are sandwiches on fresh breads and cookies the size of a kindergartner's hands. Outdoor seating is in a beautiful garden with a fountain and an overhead trellis with hanging grape vines.

MCI CENTER

One reason to visit this center of activity is to see a Washington Wizards, Capitals, or Mystics (women's basketball) game or another kid-oriented event, including ice-skating extravaganzas or the circus. But there are two other reasons to come to the crossroads of Metro's red, green, and yellow lines, and they're available year-round.

At the Discovery Channel Store: Destination Washington, DC, you and your child can "explore your world" (and beyond) on three floors: oceans and fossils on the first floor; land, culture, and animals on the second; and sky and space on the third. Highlights include the front of a real B-25 bomber, a life-size T-rex cast, and interactive computer games. Of course, intermingled among the displays are tons of stuff to buy, including telescopes, science kits, travel gear, rain-forest products, and Discovery Channel CD/ROMS.

Sports fans head to the MCI National Sports Gallery, where they can grip the Babe's bat or put on a helmet to hear a play called in a life-size football huddle. Even more exciting are

HEY, KIDS! Did you know that the T-rex in the Discovery Channel Store is 20 feet tall and 42 feet long and has 12-inch teeth? That's quite a bit bigger than the late basketball legend Wilt Chamberlain, who was a mere 7'2" and whose teeth were roughly the same size as yours! Even if Chamberlain had worn stilts—his nickname was Wilt the Stilt—the T-rex would still have towered over the famous hoop star. You can see Chamberlain's Harlem Globetrotter uniform in the MCI National Sports Gallery.

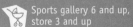

601 F St. NW. Metro: Gallery Place/Chinatown

202/628–3200; 202/661–5133 sports gallery; 202/639–0908 store

Sports gallery $5, admission with game credits $7 and up; store free

Sports gallery daily 12–6, later during games and events. Store M–Sa 10–9, Su 12–6

Sports gallery 6 and up, store 3 and up

the interactive sports zones, featuring historical artifacts and game opportunities in baseball, basketball, football, golf, hockey, skiing, soccer, and tennis. A few games can be adjusted by skill level; for example, at the baseball hitting booth, kids can slow down the action and speed up success by opting for "minor league" competition. However, most games are aimed at children old enough for organized sports. The soccer game, called Take Your Best Shot, involves kicking a tethered ball into a box below an interactive video. In the hockey game, Shot on Goal, a surly goalie dares, "Is that your best shot? This isn't tiddlywinks, man."

Kids who like to watch sports as much as play them, especially those with the gift of gab, can call play-by-plays of famous broadcasts at the American Sportscasters Hall of Fame, part of the sports gallery. Who knows? Maybe one day your child will be back at the MCI Center calling a real pro game.

KID-FRIENDLY EATS

Sports memorabilia continues at the **Gallery Café** (tel. 202/661–5133), where you can munch on ballpark fare. In Chinatown, children pat Buddha's tummy before filling their own at **Hunan Chinatown** (624 H St. NW, tel. 202/783–5858). **Tony Cheng's** (619 H St. NW, tel. 202/371–8669) offers a barbecue on the first floor and traditional fare upstairs.

KEEP IN MIND

You can see the Federal City on the silver screen at the Discovery Channel Store's theater (tel. 202/628–3200, ext. 6054). A 15-minute film, *Destination DC*, takes you on an "unofficial tour of official Washington." The movie ($2.50 adults, $1.50 kids 5–18) covers many of the historical sights reviewed in this book and lets you in on little-known historical fun facts. For example, you probably didn't know that crushed walnuts help clean and preserve the bronze statues around the capital—but you do now!

MOUNT VERNON

A visit to Mount Vernon offers much more than a chance to see George Washington's elegant and stately mansion. Depending on the time of year, your kids may dig for archaeological artifacts, ride wagons, sample hoe cakes cooked over an open fire, hike nature trails, learn songs that slaves sang, or observe the heritage breeds of farm animals that lived here long ago.

Tours of Washington's home and three gardens are self-guided. Historic interpreters throughout the house answer questions and give you a sense of our country's first president. Be sure to tell your children to look up on the ceiling in the first room to find pictures of farm tools. Upstairs the beds may look small, but that's an optical illusion resulting from being high off the ground. The shortest mattress is 6'3", a tad longer than the general himself. Perhaps more interesting to kids than the house are a dozen meticulously restored outbuildings, including a major greenhouse, a kitchen, stables, and slave quarters.

HEY, KIDS! Did you know that George Washington is the only U.S. President who did not live in the White House? During Washington's administration, the nation's capital was first in New York and then in Philadelphia. He oversaw the creation of Washington, D.C., including the White House, but never lived there. For more Washington trivia, write to the Mount Vernon Education Department (Box 110, Mount Vernon, VA 22121) for a free copy of the brochure "Rare Facts. Curious Truths."

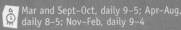
From Memorial Day to Labor Day, the Hands-on History tent (open daily 10–1) lets kids learn about 18th-century life the old-fashioned way. They can card and spin wool, construct wooden buckets, dress in period clothing, play hoops, and harness a fiberglass mule named Nellie. They can even crawl into a Revolutionary War tent full of soldiers' gear and see how they measure up to a life-size likeness of the 6'2", 190-pound Washington.

From March to November, kids get a feel for Colonial farm life at the *George Washington: Pioneer Farmer* exhibit, which has a full-size reproduction of Washington's 16-side barn. Depending on the day's activities, youngsters may crack corn, build a fence, hoe the fields, or dig for real potatoes. Special events include sheep shearing in May and plowing in June. No matter what time of year you visit Mount Vernon, pick up an Adventure Map. The real treasure is that kids learn about the father of our country.

KEEP IN MIND
Mount Vernon is the second-most-popular historic home in the country. (The White House is the first.) Tourists pull up by the busload during spring and summer. To beat the crowds, arrive in early morning or at around 3 PM, but keep in mind that the grounds close at 5.

KID-FRIENDLY EATS To protect Mount Vernon from damage and litter, food and beverages are not permitted on the grounds. Just outside the main gate you'll find a snack bar called the **Quick Bite,** which has picnic tables, and the **Mount Vernon Inn** (tel. 703/780–0011). For a taste of Colonial life, try hoe cakes or peanut and chestnut soup; more modern meals, such as chicken fingers and hamburgers for kids, are also served.

NATIONAL AIR AND SPACE MUSEUM

There's a good reason why this place is up, up, and away the most popular museum in the world: Kids love it. The 23 galleries here tell the story of aviation from the earliest human attempts at flight. Suspended from the ceiling like plastic models in a child's room are dozens of aircraft, including the actual Wright 1903 Flyer that Orville Wright piloted over the sands of Kitty Hawk, Charles Lindbergh's *Spirit of St. Louis,* the X-1 rocket plane in which Chuck Yeager broke the sound barrier, and the X-15, the fastest plane ever built.

Kids like walking through the backup model of the *Skylab* orbital workshop to see how astronauts live (in quarters as cramped as a child's messy bedroom). At the How Things Fly gallery, children sit in a real Cessna 150 cockpit, "perform" experiments in mid-air, and see wind-tunnel demonstrations. An activity board at the gallery entrance lists times for such family favorites as Flights of Fancy storytelling (ages 3–7), paper airplane contests, and demonstrations by museum "Explainers," high school and college students who encourage kids to participate.

HEY, KIDS!

You're one in a million. . . . Make that 9 or 10 million—annual visitors, that is. The world's most popular museum, it's also thought to be earth's most visited building. But don't feel insignificant. Our sun may be one of many billions of stars, but look how important it is.

KEEP IN MIND The museum is large (three blocks) and popular. To avoid crowds, go early on a weekday morning. Consider dressing your children in identical colors so that you can spot them easily. Also, review safety rules ahead of time, and point out what the guards are wearing (white shirts, navy slacks, and hats) so your children know whom to turn to if they get lost.

Jefferson Dr. or Independence Ave. and
6th St. SW. Metro: L'Enfant Plaza

 Free

 Daily 10–5:30

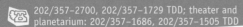 202/357-2700, 202/357-1729 TDD; theater and
planetarium: 202/357-1686, 202/357-1505 TDD

3 and up

Don't let long lines deter you from seeing a show in the five-story Samuel P. Langley Theater. IMAX films like *To Fly!* (kids' favorite) make you feel you've left the ground. Strollers aren't allowed at the movies, but then kids under 4 may find the noise and larger-than-life images frightening anyway.

For a look at the final frontier, check out the Albert Einstein Planetarium. "Sky Quest," for children 6–11, is shown at 11 and 1. "And a Star to Steer Her By," for space cadets 10 and up, airs throughout the day. "The Stars Tonight," for star gazers 6 and up, discusses at 3 PM what you can expect to see that night. Films and planetarium shows sell out quickly, so buy tickets upon arrival (or up to two weeks in advance).

When you're ready to get back down to earth, touch the moon rock at the Mall exit, one of only three on the planet you can touch.

KID-FRIENDLY EATS Two restaurants are at the museum's eastern end: The **Wright Place** (tel. 202/371-8777) offers table service and takes reservations, and the **Flight Line** is a cafeteria with windows overlooking the U.S. Capitol, the Mall, and the National Gallery of Art. Each has a large selection, but lines can be long. If you want a treat to take home, three gift shops sell flight-related merchandise, including freeze-dried astronaut food.

NATIONAL AQUARIUM

The basement of the Department of Commerce building is a strange address for a tourist attraction, but that's where you'll find the world's third-oldest public aquarium. Since the 1870s, it has housed interesting sea creatures, including a two-headed diamond terrapin in the 1940s, whose two heads would compete for the same morsel of food. The aquarium's oldest resident, an alligator gar, has been here since the 1950s.

Frankly, the Age of Aquariums has left this one behind mammoth modern aquariums—especially its more famous stepsister in Baltimore. But if you're in the District, aren't expecting state-of-the-art displays, and want a cool place to relax, this national aquarium is worth a stop. Though its modesty may disappoint older kids looking for a big splash, it's great for children young enough to enjoy pet goldfish. For parents of tots, its small size is a plus.

You can circle the museum twice in about 45 minutes. Aisles are wide enough for double strollers, and the aquarium isn't generally crowded. Nevertheless, more than 250 species and

HEY, KIDS! Things aren't always what they seem. The horseshoe crab isn't really a crab at all. It's more closely related to a spider. And the green moray eel is actually blue with a yellow coating that protects it from disease and infection. But one thing is as it appears. A moray's menacing-looking mouth does deliver a very fierce bite. But then anyone who re- members the sinister Flotsam and Jetsam from *The Little Mermaid* knows they're hardly the warm and fuzzy type.

 14th St. and Constitution Ave. NW.
Metro: Federal Triangle

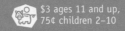 $3 ages 11 and up,
75¢ children 2–10

 Daily 9–5

202/482-2826

2 and up

1,700 specimens of aquatic life, including American alligators, nurse sharks, spiny lobsters, flashlight fish, clownfish, flesh-chomping piranhas, and their seaworthy mates swim here. Animals live in traditional numbered rectangular tanks, though some of the signage is missing, which frustrates older children who want to know the creatures' names. Tank 44 challenges kids to find 20 fish camouflaged among the aquatic plants. In the touch pool, kids can handle horseshoe crabs, hermit crabs, pencil sea urchins, and conchs.

Special events are held throughout the year. On Shark Day, you can watch a shark dissection. During SOS (Save Our Sea Creatures Day), conservation experts answer kids' questions and give advice on how they can save the world— or at least a fish. The aquarium lost government funding in 1982 and almost closed, but a group of fish-lovers formed a nonprofit group to save it. As you leave, consider making a donation to keep the aquarium afloat.

KID-FRIENDLY EATS Sharks are fed at 2 on Monday, Wednesday, and Saturday. Piranhas are fed at 2 on Tuesday, Thursday, and Sunday. People can catch a bite to eat at any time at food courts in the lower level of the **Ronald Reagan Building** (1300 Pennsylvania Ave. NW, tel. 202/312–1399) or the top level of **The Shops** (see the White House).

KEEP IN MIND If this National Aquarium only whets your child's appetite for more fish, you may wish to check out the much larger and glitzier National Aquarium in Baltimore (Pier 3, tel. 410/576–3810). An hour's drive from D.C. in non-rush-hour traffic, it's Maryland's number one tourist attraction. But be warned: It's more expensive and more crowded than Washington's aquarium, and strollers are not permitted. After a day among the hordes, you may wish you'd put glow-in-the-dark tape on your kids' shoes to keep track of them.

NATIONAL ARBORETUM

How does your garden grow? Here the garden grows with priceless, 350-year-old trees smaller than a 2-year-old, herbs, an aquatic garden, and 15,000 magnificent azaleas, peonies, and day lilies. The arboretum has two entrances: New York Avenue and R Street, off Bladensburg Road. Whichever you choose, your first stop should be the administration building, where you'll see speckled, bright orange koi flourishing in the surrounding pool. Some are as long as a child's arm, others as little as a finger. Pick up a map inside. You'll need it. Almost 10 miles of winding roads cover 444 acres of botanical masterpieces.

Make sure you visit the National Bonsai and Penjing Museum. (In China tray landscapes are called penjing, and in Japan artistic potted plants are bonsai.) These arts have been depicted in Chinese paintings as early as the 6th century. The idea is simple: Just as you get your hair cut to achieve a desired look, so these trees are trimmed for a desired look, which varies by species. The trees are worth, "about as much as your children," according to the man in charge, Warren Hill. Many have been nurtured for generations, and some were

HEY, KIDS!

Do you know your state tree? At the National Grove of State Trees, you can search for the official trees of all 50 states and the District of Columbia. Pick up a state tree list at the administration building. Don't look for markers on the ground; identification tags hang from the branches.

KEEP IN MIND You may wish to drive, bike, walk, or do a little of each around the arboretum. Walking is pleasant, especially with a stroller, but you can't cover much ground. You'll get farther biking, and racks for locking your bicycle are scattered about the collection. Driving is slow—the speed limit is 20 mph and enforced—but you can park at each garden/museum within the arboretum and then walk around. On weekends between April and mid-October, you can take a 40-minute narrated tram ride.

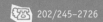
gifts to presidents. Your children might enjoy wandering through outdoor rooms in search of the oldest trees, the smallest trees, or those with interesting trunks.

Follow your nose to the National Herb Garden, where herbs from around the world are arranged. Experience aloe, oregano, wild strawberries, licorice, English lavender, and ginger. Hundreds of heritage roses also bloom here. Fruits, vegetables, and flowers thrive in the Youth Garden, planted by schoolkids, who share what they grow with the homeless.

But plants aren't the only things jutting out from the earth here. Twenty-two sandstone Corinthian columns that once stood at the east portico of the U.S. Capitol are set in a rectangle in a meadow. Within them is a fountain, where water flows into a reflecting pool. It's a serene and pleasant place, one where your kids can be engaged for hours.

KID-FRIENDLY EATS Alas, there's no food for sale here, and you're certainly not allowed to pick the fruits, vegetables, or herbs, no matter how tempting they appear. (Think the Garden of Eden.) However, you can bring your own and take advantage of picnic tables under the state trees.

NATIONAL BUILDING MUSEUM

Budding builders and architects are awed by this monumental redbrick building. The Great Hall, site of many inaugural balls, is 15 stories tall and as long as a football field. Eight 75-foot Corinthian columns are among the world's largest. Though they look like marble, each is made of 75,000 bricks, covered with plaster and marbleized.

After viewing the breathtaking hall, head upstairs to the Washington: Symbol and City exhibit, where your children can handle plastic models of the Capitol, White House, Washington Monument, and Lincoln Memorial. Through interactive displays, they can create their own row houses by flipping three-dimensional panels and can answer architectural questions on a board that lights up when correct answers are given. They can even choose their favorite design from among those originally submitted for the Washington Monument. Special exhibits change as often as 10 times per year, but all focus on the people, processes, or materials that create buildings and other "places." Recent exhibits have explored air-conditioning, architecture in the 21st century, and tools as art.

HEY, KIDS! The Big Bad Wolf won't blow this house down! More than 15 million bricks make up this building, designed by Civil War veteran Montgomery Meigs and constructed from 1882 to 1887. Bricks protect against fire, important since the building housed the records and offices of the Pension Bureau—the agency that sent checks to disabled veterans and soldiers' widows. Outside, a 1,200-foot frieze (pronounced "freeze") depicts many military units. Can you find three ways people traveled on this decorative band?

So why don't buildings fall down? Your children (and you) can learn why at the free, drop-in program "Arches and Trusses: The Tension Builds," held Saturday at 2:30. As part of the program, children participate in hands-on demonstrations, learning about compression by squeezing squishy balls and tension by stretching rubber bands. They can also put their many years of block-building experience to work as they create buildings out of the museum's "demonstration bricks" for an appreciative audience. Other family programs, which include building-block contests, making gingerbread houses, and dome construction, require reservations; some are free, and most are under $10.

To get the most from the museum whenever you visit, pick up a printed activity guide (free with a donation) at the front desk. The guide helps kids explore the museum—the museum's largest artifact—at their own pace and includes activities that can be done in the museum and at home.

KID-FRIENDLY EATS If your kids have built up an appetite, visit the museum's **Blueprints Café** (tel. 202/504–2737). Order such cleverly named sandwiches as the Frank Lloyd Wright, built on a foundation of turkey and baguette with a plaster of herb mayo, cantilevered apples, all leveled with melted cheddar. Other menu additions are salads, quiche, and soup.

KEEP IN MIND The National Building Museum's extensive school programs (also available to other groups, like scout troops) complement curricula in social studies, geography, industrial arts, science, art, math, and history. Under the guidance of the museum's educators, students may plan an imaginary town, build model bridges, or assemble an 8' x 11' house from the ground up with foundations, wall frames, and trusses. Most programs cost a dollar or two for each student. For information, call the museum's education department.

NATIONAL CAPITAL TROLLEY MUSEUM

What small child doesn't love trains? And what small child who loves trains doesn't love trolleys? You can test this hypothesis at this combination trolley trip and museum. The 20-minute voyage covers 1¾ miles of track through a wooded area. Occasionally, passengers see deer, fox, rabbits, and groundhogs, but kids are usually content just watching the trolley itself.

Also called streetcars, trolleys were first used in Washington, D.C., during the Lincoln administration to accommodate the influx of people during the Civil War. Early streetcars were drawn by horses, but these were replaced by cable cars and ultimately by electric cars, which skimmed fast and smooth along the tracks. (Today's cars go about 25 mph, but they once went up to 45 mph outside the city.) The last Washington trolleys ran during the Kennedy administration. In fact, you might be riding in one of these last cars or in any of five others from elsewhere. The museum's collection comprises 17 cars, which are all brought out on the third Sunday in April for the Cavalcade of Cars and the third Sunday in October for the Fall Open House. Both events also feature other attractions, such as a barbershop quartet

HEY, KIDS!

Each conductor had a hole punch with a different shape. Some looked like stars or zigzags. That way if a passenger had a complaint, the person who punched the ticket could be identified. Today's operators still have different shaped punches. What do the punches on your ticket look like?

KEEP IN MIND The biggest trolley trick for parents of toddlers is keeping them safely seated during the short ride. Luckily, the trolley makes one stop en route, when kids can get up and walk around. This is also when enthusiastic volunteers give brief trolley talks and answer questions. Often some of the passengers will remember riding the trolley when they were kids.

1313 Bonifant Rd., between Layhill Rd. and New Hampshire Ave., Wheaton, MD

 Jan–mid-Nov, Sa–Su 12–5, plus Th–F 10–2 mid-Mar–mid-May and early Oct–mid-Nov and Th–F 11–3 mid-June–mid-Aug; Dec, Sa–Su 5–9

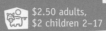 301/384–6088 $2.50 adults, $2 children 2–17 2–7 and all train lovers

or scarecrow-making. During December's Holly Trolleyfest, the museum is decked in lights, and Santa greets children during the trolley stop.

Also take time to enjoy the museum, resembling an old-time railroad station. Fortunately, there's no danger of losing track of your children, as the museum occupies only 1,500 square feet. With a boost, even the smallest child can press a button sending a model trolley whizzing around in a case depicting Connecticut Avenue in the early 1930s. Older kids and parents can learn the parts of a trolley and the history of D.C. trolleys through interactive computers.

Trolley memorabilia, *Thomas the Tank Engine* books, and other train-related merchandise are available in the shop. A free "Little Folks Guide to the Trolley Museum" handout and the trolley tickets themselves provide nice mementos that can be used to play trolley at home.

KID-FRIENDLY EATS Food and drink aren't allowed in the museum or on the cars, but there are picnic tables behind the museum. Families can be choosy at the Layhill Shopping Center (Layhill and Bel Pre Rds.), where they'll find typical American food and crayons at the **Layhill Cafe** (tel. 301/598–7772), Italian fare and video games at **Sole d' Italia** (tel. 301/598–6660), and Chinese food at **Lee's Kitchen** (tel. 301/598–4810).

NATIONAL GALLERY OF ART

Some kids think it looks like a bird, others a plane, but most agree it's super. Looming as large as a small aircraft, a mobile by Alexander Calder soars overhead in the East Building atrium here. It's just one of the works that fascinate kids at this art museum, one of the world's most visited. The gallery comprises two very different buildings and a sculpture garden. The airy and spacious East Building's modern art—by Picasso, Matisse, Miró, and others—appeals to children, as does the exterior of the I. M. Pei–designed trapezoidal structure. In fact, since its 1978 opening, the bladelike southwest corner has been darkened and polished smooth by thousands of hands irresistibly drawn to touch it.

In the neoclassical West Building, over 100 galleries contain 13th- to 20th-century works. Though art lovers easily spend all day here, most little children last about an hour. (Strollers are available at both buildings' entrances.) Students of architecture may notice that the building's dome shape resembles the Jefferson Memorial. Both buildings were designed by John Russell Pope and opened in the early 1940s.

HEY, KIDS! Do you know an old lady who swallowed a spider? Check out the massive *Spider* by Louise Bourgeois in the sculpture garden here. It's large enough to frighten even the bravest Miss Muffet! After you find the spider, can you locate the rabbit? Unlike Peter Rabbit or the March Hare in *Alice and Wonderland,* the rabbit in *Thinker on the Rock,* by Barry Flanagan, doesn't appear cunning or curious. He looks contemplative. What do you suppose he's thinking about?

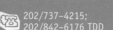 4th St. and Constitution Ave. NW. Metro: Judiciary Square, Archives, Smithsonian

 Free

 M–Sa 10–5, Su 11–6

202/737–4215;
202/842–6176 TDD

4 and up

In 1999, the gallery opened a dynamic sculpture garden with more than a dozen works spread around a fountain that transforms into an ice rink in winter. The only sculpture kids (or adults) can touch is Scott Burton's *Six-Part Seating,* with its polished granite chairs. Still, the meandering paths provide unexpected treasures. Kids like to look through the window of Roy Lichtenstein's *House I.* Claes Oldenburg and Coosje van Bruggen's mammoth *Typewriter Eraser, Scale X* will look foreign to kids born in the computer age. Ask your kids to guess what it is!

Yes, visiting here will reassure you that you're exposing your children to sophisticated art and architecture and hopefully spark an interest in them. But don't be surprised if the highlight of their experience is tossing pennies into the sculpture garden's fountain or riding the moving walkway in the underground tunnel connecting the two buildings.

KID-FRIENDLY EATS The gallery has five options: **On the Concourse,** a buffet, serves breakfast and pizza or sandwich lunches; the **Espresso Bar** sells light snacks. In the West Building, the **Garden Cafe** (tel. 202/216–2494) features entrées related to current exhibitions. In the East Building, the **Terrace Café** (tel. 202/216–2492) overlooks the Mall. Or why not eat on the sculpture garden's camel-back sofas?

KEEP IN MIND Family programs (registration required) are held on weekends year-round. Including tours and hands-on activities, they last 1½ hours for 4–5 year olds and 2 hours for 6–13 year olds. Activities may include taking Polaroids, painting, sculpting, or making collages. If you'd rather go it alone, start in the Micro Gallery, where you can preview works by computer and then print out a personalized map. You may also borrow a "Family Guide" from the front desk or buy one ($2.50) from the Children's Shop.

NATIONAL GEOGRAPHIC'S
EXPLORERS HALL

The National Geographic Society's famous yellow-bordered magazine—found in doctor's offices, family rooms, and attics nationwide—is not exactly for kids. Yet Explorers Hall brings the magazine to life for them. In the hall's many sections, the planet's wonders are brought closer, showing kids that it is indeed a small world after all.

The hall's permanent exhibits are housed in the building's north end, in what's called Geographica. Here you can wave your hand through a tornado or find out what the weather is like in West Africa or what time it is in Turkey. Video touch screens explain various geographic concepts and then quiz you on what you've learned. In the interactive aquarium, images of fish seemingly swim in space. Reach out to touch one and the fish disappears, but a voice then describes the fish.

Geographica is also the home of a 5'4" skeletal head (with serrated teeth) of a *Carcharodontosaurus,* a dinosaur that rivals the better-known T-rex in stature. And in case

HEY, KIDS!
While you can't get your picture on the cover of *Rolling Stone*, you can see your face on *National Geographic*. Postcard-size pictures ($5) can be made at In the Picture, and you can even choose the background: at the White House or the pyramids, on the moon, or with a seal.

KEEP IN MIND Although all exhibits are on one floor, the hall is divided into many sections, so you'll need to be vigilant about watching children who tend to wander off. If you do get separated, a good meeting place is the reception desk, but a better reason to visit the desk is to learn about Passport Fridays, free live demonstrations held sometime between 10 and 2. At least once a month the program is Scales and Tails, a live bird and reptile show and informal discussion on threatened and endangered species.

the size of the dinosaur doesn't impress your kids, perhaps the Goliath frog will. The largest of the world's more than 250 frog species, it weighs in at 7 pounds, the size of an average newborn baby.

However, the most dramatic events take place in Earth Station One, a 72-seat amphitheater that sends the audience on a journey around the world. By pushing buttons on pads in front of their seats, viewers answer questions from a "pilot" narrator. Kids get immediate feedback as the audience's responses are instantly tallied on video screens. The centerpiece here is the world's largest freestanding globe, 11 feet in diameter and hand-painted, which floats and spins on a cushion of air, showing off different features of the planet.

The hall's south end is devoted to changing exhibits that stretch the definition of geography well beyond state capitals. Recent exhibits have explored cats, water, and pirates . . . in other words, anything under the sun.

KID-FRIENDLY EATS In a neighborhood catering to businesspeople, you won't find high chairs, but you will find reasonable prices. At **Café LA** (1719 M St. NW, tel. 202/775–1652), food is bought by the pound. The **California Grill** (1720 M St. NW, tel. 202/463– 4200) is a self-service restaurant specializing in Mexican and American cuisine. At the **Mudd House** (1724 M St. NW, tel. 202/822–8455), parents sip specialty coffees while kids enjoy hot chocolate.

NATIONAL MUSEUM OF AFRICAN ART

Kids can really relate to the art at this museum. Perhaps it's because every child has turned a paper plate into a mask or strung beads together to make a necklace. Perhaps it's because so many of the works incorporate animals. Wander through this Smithsonian museum with your child, and you'll see all sorts of African artworks: musical instruments, pottery, beaded works, sculptures, carvings, and masks and headdresses made to entertain or personify characters or animals. One tall mask from Zaire, for example, is made of painted woods and raffia and was worn at rituals celebrating the arrival of the new moon. Jewelry on display is made of such materials as beads, woods, fiber, bronze, ivory, and fired clay.

One of the best ways to learn about the arts and cultures of Africa is through the AfriKid Art programs, aimed at kids 4 and up. At drop-in workshops (most of which are free), children are taught about the materials, colors, animals, and countries of origin of items in the permanent collection, such as a colorful beaded crown or a life-size figure of a man. They may also be asked to answer questions like, "How would you describe the object to someone who couldn't

HEY, KIDS! Create your own African treasure hunt. Find the Baga mask weighing 92 pounds (not recommended for Halloween) or the pipe carved into a train. Hunt down a bird perched on an ivory spoon or the African "pillow"—actually a carved wooden headrest shaped like an elephant—and decide if it looks comfortable. What about the enormous hammered gold earrings, which are frequently supported by a leather strap? If you need help finding any items, ask at the information desk.

950 Independence Ave. SW. Metro: Smithsonian

 Free

 Daily 10–5:30

202/357–2700, 202/357–4814 TDD

4 and up

see it?" or "How do you think it would feel to wear this hat?" After touring the gallery, kids pursue an activity, such as beading, weaving, or hat making, and can take their masterpiece home as a souvenir.

The museum also has storytelling sessions, during which folktales are often combined with music and dance to bring legends from the African continent to life for North American kids. And in the true tradition of African storytelling, the audience frequently chimes in.

To help in your exploration, pick up a copy of "Images of Power and Identity," a family guide to the permanent collection. It might challenge you and your kids to count the number of equestrian figures in the gallery or identify the artist who made a large palace door. It should also increase your enjoyment.

KID-FRIENDLY EATS The National Air and Space Museum, the National Museum of Natural History, and the National Museum of American History have on-site restaurants (*see listings*).

KEEP IN MIND To expand your children's global view even further, walk about 100 paces west through the Enid A. Haupt Garden or just open the door at the end of the Art of the Personal Object gallery, and you'll be in the Sackler Gallery (*see below*), which is connected to the Freer Gallery of Art. The emphasis at these nearby museums is on another continent altogether: Asia.

NATIONAL MUSEUM OF AMERICAN HISTORY

Oh say, can you see the flag that inspired "The Star-Spangled Banner," Oscar the Grouch, an original teddy bear from 1903, first ladies' inaugural gowns, and an old Indy 500 race car? You can, and you can see lots more American memorabilia at this museum, whose incredible diversity of artifacts gave it the nickname "the nation's attic."

Exhibits on the first of three floors emphasize the history of science and technology and include such items as farm machines, antique automobiles, early phonographs, and a 280-ton steam locomotive. Two *Jurassic Park* eggs and an orange-masked Teenage Mutant Ninja Turtle are in the Science in American Life exhibit. The second floor is devoted to U.S. social and political history and has an exhibit on everyday American life just after the Revolution. The third floor's Icons of American Pop Culture displays items that may be quite familiar to kids, including ruby slippers from the *Wizard of Oz,* Michael Jordan's jersey from the 1996 NBA finals, and Indiana Jones's jacket and hat. The floor also features money, graphic arts, musical instruments, photography, and news reporting.

KEEP IN MIND During busy times, passes are required for both hands-on rooms. Passes are free and may be picked up on a first-come, first-served basis at the door to each room. They entitle you to stay for a ½ hour.

HEY, KIDS! Watch through a floor-to-ceiling window as conservators work to preserve the flag that inspired the Francis Scott Key poem that became our national anthem. (The masks protect the flag from bacteria and conservators from microscopic dust.) Conservation of the three-story flag—sewn in 1813 by Mary Pickersgill and her 13-year-old daughter Caroline for $405.90—should continue until 2002. Its 15 stars and stripes represented the states at the time.

14th St. and Constitution Ave.
SW. Metro: Smithsonian

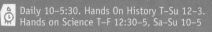 Daily 10–5:30. Hands On History T–Su 12–3.
Hands on Science T–F 12:30–5, Sa–Su 10–5

202/357–2700

 Free

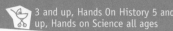 3 and up, Hands On History 5 and
up, Hands on Science all ages

For a more interactive visit, children and adults should stop at two places: In the Hands On History Room, you can straddle a high-wheeler, send messages by telegraph, gin cotton, or say hello in Cherokee. In the Hands on Science Room, kids of all ages use lasers to measure distance, unravel the mysteries of DNA, and conduct tests for water pollutants as scientists did in the 1880s.

Request one of the free "Hunt for History" guides, for kids ages 6–9 and 10–13, at an information desk. The Peanuts characters take children on a scavenger hunt throughout the museum, during which they'll learn what's inside the original White House elevator (a pony) and who sank the gunboat *Philadelphia* in 1776 (the British).

As in their own attic at home, kids can stay amused for hours as they discover remarkable treasures. Luckily it's not as dusty.

KID-FRIENDLY EATS If your kids are screaming for ice cream, take a break at the museum's **Palm Court** (tel. 202/357–1832), whose decor makes it feel like a Victorian-style ice-cream parlor. You can get a sandwich or soup, and then, if you've saved room, you can watch as they make you a sweet treat—perhaps a sundae, ice-cream float, milk shake, or a banana split so huge that two children (maybe even four) can split it.

B oys and girls who want real goose bumps or who have an interest in a medical career can find lots of really cool stuff at this medical museum that depicts the fight against injury and disease. Because some of the exhibits are fairly graphic (e.g., wax surgical models, organs in formaldehyde), the museum may not be suitable for the squeamish.

At the Pregnancy exhibit, kids can put on a garment that makes them appear pregnant and can then attempt to tie their shoes, perhaps instilling some small appreciation for what their mother went through. At the Human Body exhibit, they can get an up-close look at human organs, like livers, stomachs, lungs, and kidneys. Some organs are "plastinated"—preserved in plastic so they can be held—and injected with blue and red dyes so arteries can be distinguished from veins. All are real.

At still other exhibits, your children can learn about the evolution of the microscope, view the human body from a 3-D perspective at an interactive computer station, discover why

HEY, KIDS! Talk about a bizarre story. During the Battle of Gettysburg, a 12-pound cannonball splintered the right leg of Civil War General Daniel E. Sickles. After it was amputated, he sent the leg to this museum, then known as the Army Medical Museum, where it's still on display, along with a picture of the general as an amputee. Incidentally, the eccentric General Sickles used to visit his leg here and would sometimes bring friends to see it.

disease killed more soldiers than bullets during the Civil War, and look at early medical instruments used in skull surgery and dentistry. Check out the turnkey, a large old-fashioned door key redesigned with a hook to extract molars. Then look at the leeches. They were used centuries ago to treat diseases. There's lots to see here to make everyone grateful for modern medicine.

Teens may view a video made by their peers about HIV testing and then test their own knowledge of AIDS, using computer games. When the Discovery Cart is open (weekends and holidays 2–4), brave ones can touch a real human brain, peer through a microscope at a detached retina, and use forensic methods to examine bones for clues about height, age, and gender. But even if the museum's displays of how our bodies work don't get your youngsters interested in medicine, they may at least be encouraged—or even frightened—into taking steps to maintain or improve healthful habits.

KID-FRIENDLY EATS Grab lunch (weekdays) at the **American Registry of Pathology Cafeteria** (Building 54, tel. 202/782–2563). For greater selection and low prices, walk to the **Walter Reed Hospital Cafeteria** (Building 2, tel. 202/782–3501). **Crisfield** (8012 Georgia Ave., Silver Spring, tel. 301/589–1306) has great inexpensive seafood.

KEEP IN MIND If you're bringing a younger sibling (ages 4–7) with you, ask for a Discovery Box at the information desk. They'll have four boxes to choose from: eyesight, pregnancy, the human body, and nutrition. The human body box includes a life-size doll with layers that can be peeled away to see inside the body. The pregnancy box helps to teach kids why they have a belly button. Each of the boxes includes a take-home worksheet that adds to the learning fun.

NATIONAL MUSEUM OF NATURAL HISTORY

S ay hello to Henry. One of the largest elephants ever found in the world, this stuffed beast has greeted generations of kids in the rotunda of this huge museum, which is dedicated to natural wonders of the world, both big and small. From the marble floor of the rotunda, you can look up at banners announcing the exhibits and decide where you want to go.

In the popular Dinosaur Hall, fossilized skeletons range from a 90-foot-long diplodocus to a tiny *Thesalorsaurus neglectus* (so named because its bones sat for years in a museum drawer before being reassembled). The Hall of Mammals is closed for renovations until 2003, but you can still check out the mighty but endangered tiger and learn about its life and efforts to protect it.

At the African Voices exhibit, kids can see dolls from around the continent (many made by children), view 18 types of currency, and listen to African sounds on music wands, while their older siblings design mud cloth on the computer. (It's a good thing it's done on

HEY, KIDS!

In the O. Orkin Insect Zoo, you'll see ants that cut leaves, beetles that spray their enemies, and roaches that freak out grown-ups. Believe it or not, though, in some parts of the world insects are readily eaten. Grasshoppers are the most commonly consumed, but wasps have the highest protein content.

KEEP IN MIND
Children explore with their hands in the Discovery Room. (In the spring and summer, free passes are distributed starting at 11:45 on weekdays and 10:15 weekends.) In 2002 an expanded version is moving to the new Discovery Center, where you'll already find the 487-seat Samuel C. Johnson Theater and its IMAX films. For 3-D flicks, you get to don oversize glasses. The museum's extensive gift shop is full of books, model dinosaurs, and educational games that kids love and parents approve.

Constitution Ave. and 10th St. NW.
Metro: Smithsonian

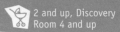 Free

202/357-2700

Daily 10–5:30. Discovery Room T–F 12–2:30,
Sa–Su 10:30–3:30

2 and up, Discovery
Room 4 and up

the computer, because the actual process—using mud and dyes to create patterns—is quite messy.) Older children may also enjoy the Janet Annenberg Hooker Hall of Geology, Gems & Minerals, which takes rock collecting to new heights and includes a neat exhibit on volcanoes and earthquakes. The Hope Diamond is also here, slowly rotating in a four-sided glass case. The most-visited museum object in the world, it's even more popular than the *Mona Lisa!*

Not everything in the museum is dead or inanimate, though. For some action, take your kids to the second floor's O. Orkin Insect Zoo, home to live ants, bees, centipedes, tarantulas, roaches as large as mice, and other critters you wouldn't want in your house. After viewing these creepy creatures, young bug fanciers can act the part by crawling through a model of an African termite mound.

From tiny to tremendous, the natural wonders at this natural history museum will amuse your own little wonder and you.

KID-FRIENDLY EATS Tarantula feedings take place in the insect zoo at 10:30, 11:30, and 1:30 Tuesday through Friday and a few times a day on weekends. (Check at the information desk in the rotunda for a schedule.) Whereas the tarantulas' meal plan consists of the same old thing every day (crickets), you have lots of choices in the museum's 600-seat **Atrium Café,** in the new Discovery Center. Sorry, no crickets.

NATIONAL MUSEUM OF WOMEN
IN THE ARTS

E very day is International Women's Day at this beautifully restored 1907 Renaissance Revival building, showcasing works by prominent female artists from the Renaissance to the present. Ironically, it was once a men-only Masonic temple. Today in addition to traveling shows, the museum houses a permanent collection including paintings, drawings, sculpture, prints, and photographs by such artists as Helen Frankenthaller, Mary Cassatt, Gabrielle Münter, and Frida Kahlo.

As at many art museums, it's not easy to know what children will like. Frida Baranek's nonobjective sculpture has kids talking. Some youngsters think this untitled work looks like a bird's nest or a huge tumbleweed that moves, albeit subtly. Others say it reminds them of a bad hair day. Nineteenth-century French artist Rosa Bonheur is known for imaginative animal paintings, filled with rich and realistic textures. Teens may enjoy contrasting their practical clothes (some more practical than others) with the ornate Renaissance-era clothing of the young woman in Lavinia Fontana's *Portrait of a Noblewoman* (1580).

HEY, KIDS!
Do you like bugs? Does your mom? When Maria Sibylla Merian (born 1647) was about 14 years old, she started collecting, studying, and drawing insects. You can see Maria Merian's highly descriptive etchings and watercolors at the museum.

KEEP IN MIND Once a year, the museum is transformed from formal to fun as women and men, girls and boys gather here for music, dancing, hands-on crafts, storytelling, and more at the museum's annual Family Festival. Usually celebrating another culture, the event is generally held in early spring, but the date varies because the festival is tied in with special exhibits. By October, the museum staff should be able to tell you when the next Family Festival will be held.

Children can start on the path to artistic self-discovery by picking up a Case for Comparison box at the front desk. The instructions encourage children to think about what they look like, how they feel about themselves, and how they'd describe themselves, all while viewing works from the permanent collection. They can then draw a self-portrait incorporating artists' techniques.

Free family programs for children and role model workshops for teens are held about once a month. Reservations are a must. If you're not attending a children's program, stop by the Education Resource Center, where you can find at least one hands-on activity, and the information desk, where you can pick up not only a Case for Comparison but also an "Artventure" brochure (ages 7–12), which suggests ways to look at art through the elements of line, shape, color, and texture. Even though the artists covered at the museum are limited to women, the approach to art and the appeal to visitors are universal.

KID-FRIENDLY EATS Jukebox music and a kids' menu are part of the draw at the **Capital City Brewing Company** (1100 New York Ave. NW, tel. 202/628–2222); tours of the brewery are often available upon request. For the more adventurous eater, **Haad Thai** (1100 New York Ave. NW, tel. 202/682–1111) offers kids crispy rolls and chicken on a skewer. A bright mural set on the beaches of southern Thailand covers an entire wall.

NATIONAL POSTAL MUSEUM

Look up and see one of the first airmail planes. Look down and see floor tiles shaped like stamped envelopes. Look around and you'll see first-class opportunities for children at this Smithsonian-operated museum dedicated to our postal history.

Six major galleries highlight a range of topics, including the Colonial post, the Pony Express, mail transportation, and the beauty and lore of stamps. More than 40 interactive games and touch screens offer hands-on opportunities to learn more about mail. But the museum isn't all high-tech. One exhibit re-creates a Native American trail that postal carriers followed between New York and Boston. There aren't any signs to guide you. The only way to find the right route is to look for notches in the trees. Another exhibit celebrates the art and history of letter writing and encourages kids to write letters, but even kids too young to read or write are engaged here. Youngsters can climb aboard a stagecoach, pretend to sort mail in a railway postal car, and watch videos of famous train robberies.

KEEP IN MIND If you've grown used to the Smithsonian museums on the Mall, be prepared for a much smaller facility. You can wander through the postal museum in about 45 minutes. If you're downtown for the day, consider combining a visit here with one to the Capital Children's Museum (*see above*). And if your children were smitten by the museum's transportation-oriented exhibits or nearby Union Station, visit the Great Train Store (Union Station, tel. 202/371–2881), which has all manner of train sets, engineers' hats, and other choo-choo–related toys and books.

2 Massachusetts Ave. NE. Metro: Union Station

202/357-2700, 202/357-2020 recording, 202/357-1729 TDD

 Free

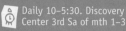 Daily 10–5:30. Discovery Center 3rd Sa of mth 1–3

3 and up

At the Discovery Center, activities are arranged in huge mailboxes by age appropriateness. While preschoolers cut and paste to make bookmarks out of canceled stamps, preteens test their knowledge of history by matching items of trivia to people portrayed on stamps.

When you're ready to leave the museum, make sure your children check out the customized postcard machine. After a postcard is addressed, the computer uses maps and sound to show how it will travel to its intended destination—anywhere in the world!

KID-FRIENDLY EATS Gettysburger Address (cheeseburger), Pentagon pizza, and presidential pasta are on the kids' menu at the **Capital City Brewery** (2 Massachusetts Ave. NE, tel. 202/842–2337), in the same building as the museum. Across the street is **Union Station** (*see* the Capital Children's Museum and D.C. Ducks), where you can choose among a huge food court and many restaurants.

HEY, KIDS! Camels, birds, reindeer, and dogs have all helped deliver the mail, but although Owney the Dog never carried any, he was still the mascot of the railway mail service in the late 19th century. Owney logged some 143,000 miles in his career and was a genuine celebrity, making appearances at dog shows and conventions. If David Letterman had been alive, Owney would no doubt have visited the *Late Show*. Thanks to taxidermy, you can actually see Owney at the museum.

NATIONAL THEATRE

Picture your average Saturday morning. Your kids are wound up and getting crazy. Fortunately, they're not the only ones acting up. Make your way to the National Theatre, one of the country's oldest theaters, and you can see children's theater groups, mimes, puppeteers, dance troupes, and magicians put on acts as part of Saturday Mornings at the National. Even firefighters and scientific experts explaining the aeronautics of yo-yos have graced Washington's oldest stage. Each Saturday brings a completely different performer.

While the National may look like it's just for kids on Saturday, at other times it hosts nationally known shows, such as *Les Misérables, Ragtime,* and *Rent*. Thankfully, it also has a mission to bring free performances to the community. In addition to its Saturday morning programs, it screens films on Monday evening during Summer Cinema at the National. Family-friendly flicks that appeal to older children have included *Back to the Future* and *Close Encounters of the Third Kind*.

HEY, KIDS!
The National is known as the Theatre of Presidents because every president since Andrew Jackson has attended at least one performance. Though there have been fires, the National has been on this spot, just three blocks from the White House, since 1835.

KEEP IN MIND Because Saturday Mornings at the National represent such an eclectic assortment of shows, chances are good that not everything will appeal to your children. Before you just show up, check the calendar of performances, available by sending a self-addressed stamped envelope to National Theatre, Saturday Mornings, at the address above. Or, if you haven't thought that far in advance, check *The Washington Post*.

Whether you're seeing a Saturday morning show or a Monday night movie, plan to arrive about 30 minutes in advance. (If you arrive too early, take the kids for a run on Freedom Plaza, across the street from the theater. Here you can see a statue of Revolutionary War hero General Casimir Pulaski, a map of D.C., and quotes about the city.) Tickets are distributed on a first-come, first-served basis.

Children sit on the floor while adults can stretch out in chairs during Saturday performances, which are held in the Helen Hayes Gallery, above the formal theater where Jerry Lewis, Pearl Bailey, and Helen Hayes herself have performed. After seeing her first play here at the age of 6, Hayes vowed to become an actress. Known as the First Lady of the American Theater, she won three Tony awards, two Oscars, an Emmy, and a Grammy. You can view her full-length portrait in the gallery that bears her name. And who knows? Your child may also be inspired to go into acting—or another performing art—after visiting the National.

KID-FRIENDLY EATS If you're heading for lunch after the 11:30 performance, you'll have lots of company at **Planet Hollywood** or the **Hard Rock Cafe** (*see* Ford's Theatre National Historic Site). For fewer crowds and less excitement, **The Shops** (*see* the White House) devotes one of its three floors to a food court.

Known more for political animals than real animals, Washington nevertheless possesses one of the world's foremost zoos. Thankfully, the residents at this Smithsonian bureau are nonpartisan. If your child just *has* to see one creature, visit it first. On busy days there may be waits at the popular animal houses, such as the Reptile Discovery Center or Amazonia's tropical rain forest. In the Great Flight Room, birds fly unrestricted, but they aren't the only animals above you. On overhead cables, orangutans swing from the Great Ape House to the Think Tank, where you can get a good look at the big apes while they get a better look at you. High-tech orangutans communicate with zookeepers using touch screens.

To see the world's fastest feline, check out the Cheetah Conservation area. To see animals with anywhere from zero to eight legs, visit the invertebrate exhibit, where octopuses, worms, cuttlefish, and giant crabs dwell. If most animals are dozing, check out the prairie dogs in the American prairie exhibit. These rambunctious rodents constantly pop in and out of their holes. Sometimes you can even hear them "bark" or make high-pitched sounds. For more

HEY, KIDS! If you thought dragons didn't exist, check out the National Zoo's version. Though the Komodo dragons here don't fly or breathe fire, these large lizards do have scaly bodies, forked tongues, and sharp claws and teeth. Young, 6-foot Kraken, hatched in 1992, now lives in the Reptile Discovery Center. Her parents live out back, where they won't embarrass her.

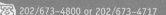

3001 Connecticut Ave. NW. Metro: Cleveland Park, Woodley Park/Zoo

 Free

202/673–4800 or 202/673–4717

May–mid-Sept, daily 6 AM–8 PM; mid-Sept–Apr, daily 6–6. Animal buildings have shorter hrs

2 and up

barking, visit the sea lions, who perform with their pals the seals daily at 11:30.

After 1972, when China gave the zoo two giant pandas, these high-profile, large-eyed creatures became its most popular residents. Alas, the last of the pair (Hsing Hsing) passed away in 1999 after a long life filled with blueberry muffins. At press time, zoo officials were seeking two new pandas, which will undoubtedly attract more headlines and visitors.

A trip to the zoo makes for an exhausting but fulfilling day. So that everyone emerges happy and healthy, watch your kids carefully; the biggest safety problem here is not animals but children wandering off. And if you want to take home more than a tired tot, stop at a gift shop for an animal facsimile that at least partly resembles the real thing.

KID-FRIENDLY EATS When your tummies start to growl, get a bite at a food kiosk or at the **Mane Restaurant,** near the Bat Cave, or the **Panda Cafe,** near—what else—the Panda House. Both restaurants serve a variety of kid-friendly food, including pizza, burgers, sandwiches, and, of course, animal crackers.

KEEP IN MIND The Cleveland Park Metro stop is a better choice than Woodley Park/Zoo, which leaves an uphill walk to the zoo but a downhill walk when you leave. Make sure your family wears comfortable shoes; the trek there is nothing compared to the walking you'll do over the zoo's 163 hilly acres. Rental strollers are available. Parking lots fill up in summer, so arrive early. Early morning (or late afternoon) is a better time to catch animals alert in summer; in cooler months, they're more active at midday.

NAVY MUSEUM

This museum is a "shore" bet for any child interested in things military. Your kids can climb on cannons, operate the barrels of anti-aircraft weapons, peer through a periscope on a submarine, and even board a space capsule. All the while, they can get a maritime perspective on American history from the American Revolution to the present, including learning about the Navy's peacetime pursuits, such as diplomacy, space flight, and humanitarian service. The Navy Museum is an especially good place to visit with a friend or relative who has served in the military.

Hands-on activities range from the no-tech, such as knot tying, to the high-tech, such as a Battle of Midway computer game in which children decipher coded messages. Free brochures listing activities for kids of all ages are available at the front desk. A kindergartner might do something as simple as drawing a hat on a sailor or connecting dots to make a plane, whereas older kids are encouraged to search for a silver sailor created from dimes or make a list of ways to prevent another world war.

KID-FRIENDLY EATS For a familiar harbor on weekdays at the Navy Yard, try **McDonald's, Subway,** or **Dunkin' Donuts.** Weekend choices are limited: McDonald's (open Saturdays March–November) or the **Catering and Conference Center cafeteria** (tel. 202/433-3041), open daily.

Washington Navy Yard, 9th and M Sts. SE

  Museum Apr–Labor Day, M–F 9–5, Sa–Su 10–5; early Sept–Mar, M–F 9–4, Sa–Su 10–5. U.S.S. *Barry* daily 10–4:30

202/433–4882 or 202/673–4800

Free

5 and up

If you call a few weeks in advance, you can arrange a special tour for your family or group. Themes include "Hats Off," during which kids learn about naval occupations by studying hats and then creating their own, and "To the Ends of the Earth and Beyond," in which youngsters study the Navy's role in polar and underwater explorations.

Outside the museum, your family can board the decommissioned U.S.S. *Barry*, a destroyer used during the Cuban Missile Crisis and the Vietnam War. Kids like the narrow halls, bunk beds, and mess hall, but they love taking the captain's wheel to "steer" the ship. Ahoy mates!

TRANSPORTA-TION The nearest Metro stop, Eastern Market, is 15–20 minutes away, and though the Navy Yard is secure, the surrounding neighborhood isn't always safe in the evening. So especially if you're planning to stay until closing, it's best to drive. From the Beltway, take I–295 south to I–395, and follow signs to the Navy Yard. Parking is free and plentiful on weekends.

HEY, KIDS! Long ago, sailors as young as 9 served aboard ship, some with their fathers. During the War of 1812, Mexican War, and Civil War, boys carrying gunpowder from the magazine to the guns—a dangerous job—were called "powder monkeys," after the real pet monkeys kept aboard. In 1755, John Barry came to America as a 10-year-old cabin boy. AKA Commodore Barry (the destroyer here was named for him), he's often considered the "Father of the American Navy."

NEWSEUM

What is news? At this $50 million, 72,000-square-foot high-tech museum, opened in 1997, you and your children can experience the story behind the stories. Founded by Allen H. Neuharth, who also founded *USA Today*, and funded by the Freedom Forum, a nonpartisan foundation dedicated to a free press and free speech, this facility is a showcase for how and why news is made.

Start at the News History Wall, which documents the newspeople, artifacts, and major stories from the first newspapers of the 1500s to the media of today. Videos and original newspaper clippings provide coverage of the Kennedy assassinations, the Vietnam War, Watergate, the *Challenger* disaster, and other major happenings.

Put your knowledge of news into action in the Interactive News Room. Through the use of computers, your children can experience what it's like to be a reporter or editor. Reporters interview doctors, students, and cheese distributors to discover why students became ill

HEY, KIDS!
What was the big news on the day you were born? Check out the popular Birthday Banner booth. For $2, you can purchase a personalized memento of that very special day.

KEEP IN MIND Because a lot of news concerns war and death, some exhibits in the Newseum may be beyond a young child's grasp or even disturbing. You can't necessarily predict when you'll come upon a graphic image, and videos constantly display today's news. Please provide guidance throughout the museum if your child is under 10 or is particularly sensitive. The way news is explained here may not be the same way you choose to explain it to your kids.

after eating toxic cheese. Editors choose which stories, photos, and headlines belong on a paper's front page.

Or your kids might like to appear on camera, reading the news, weather, or sports from a TelePrompTer in front of a choice of backdrops, including the White House, the National Zoo, and a U.S. map. Tapes of these "newscasts" are $7 each. If your little (or not-so-little) sports fans have imagined doing color commentary, they can step into a glass-enclosed sound booth to record their own versions of famous sports events, complete with the actual background sounds. An audiotape of each broadcast costs $2.

In Today's News Gallery, up-to-the-minute news is sprawled over a 126-foot-long, 10½-foot-high seamless video wall, featuring a panorama of stories from around the world. To witness tomorrow's news, kids can watch several Public Broadcasting System (PBS) programs being taped at the Newseum's studio on weekdays.

KID-FRIENDLY EATS Sandwiches and Internet access are both available at the Newseum's small **News Byte Cafe** (tel. 703/284-3786). For a more hearty meal, consider **Red Hot & Blue** (*see* Arlington National Cemetery), a Memphis-style barbecue joint known for its ribs.

OXON COVE PARK

18

I f you want to take your children back to an era when taking care of the animals meant more than walking the family dog or feeding the cat, visit this working farm (also called Oxon Hill Farm) administered by the National Park Service. On a site where the Piscataway Indians once lived, this farm has animals and equipment typical of life in a bygone era— mostly the early 19th century and later.

Down on this farm you'll find draft horses, sheep, pigs, ducks, geese, turkeys, cows, and goats— known as poor man's cows because they're capable of eating about anything and still producing milk and cheese. Children's favorite animal is Abbey, the milk cow. Like Elsie, the famous Borden cow, Abbey has horns. Most cows don't, because most modern farmers stunt their growth, as they're a hazard to farmers and other cows and they're no longer needed for protection.

HEY, KIDS!

People often think that pigs are dumb, but some farmers believe they learn quicker than horses and dogs. One popular conception that does hold true, however, concerns their trough manners. Watch as the cows' milk is delivered to them. They eat like pigs, don't you think?

KEEP IN MIND

Remind your children to move slowly near the animals and not to make any loud noises or sudden motions. Such actions are likely to startle them. And though you will no doubt get a kick out of watching your child getting a kick out of the animals, also take a moment to appreciate the panoramic view of Washington over the Potomac River.

6411 Oxon Hill Rd., Oxon Hill, MD

 Free

 Daily 8–4:30

301/839–1176

1–12

With supervision, your children may milk a cow, collect eggs warm from the nest, and—if raccoons haven't eaten it—crack and shell corn to feed the chickens. Hayrides usually depart in the afternoon.

A furnished parlor in a white farmhouse owned by the DeButts family in the early 1800s is open a few times each week. Park rangers and volunteers are usually on hand to talk about the British-born Mrs. DeButts and her views on slavery and the War of 1812. Call ahead to find out when kids can participate in daily chores and when the farmhouse is open.

Throughout the year, Oxon Hill offers free, farm-fresh programs, including sheep shearing in May, cider making in September, corn harvesting in October, and "Talking Turkey" in November. Junior ranger programs in the summertime are designed to teach 9–12 year-olds about farm life. Reservations for all programs are a must.

KID-FRIENDLY EATS For fresh food, bring your own and take advantage of picnic tables in the shade. Otherwise, your options consist of fast-food outlets along Oxon Hill Road.

PATUXENT NATIONAL WILDLIFE
VISITOR CENTER

The huge modern nature center at the Patuxent Research Refuge has enough buttons and knobs to amuse toddlers and enough gee-whiz factual information about environmental concerns to amaze teenagers. Right off the bat in the first room, older kids are challenged with such questions as "What is global warming?" and "How do we feed the world?" Younger kids may want to skip ahead to view Handles on Habitat, where they can pull a knob to see a pelican and osprey appear in the Chesapeake Bay or push a button to watch a scientist pop up with a mirror to look at birds' nests in the Hawaiian rain forest. Life-size dioramas of wild animals depict whooping cranes, timber wolves, and California sea otters swimming in kelp.

On spring–fall weekends, a 30-minute narrated tram tour runs through the refuge's meadows, forests, and wetlands, weather permitting. Though the narrator's commentary about wildlife management may be too advanced for your children, they probably will find the ride thrilling enough. Free nature movies are shown most weekends at 11, 12:30, 2, and 3:30.

KEEP IN MIND You may be tempted to leave most of your cash at home since, with the exception of the tram ride, all activities are free. However, bring a little money for the Wildlife Images Bookstore, which sells some interesting children's merchandise at reasonable prices. Your children might like some tattoos, stickers, rubber creatures, posters, or playing cards with pictures of endangered animals on them. Profits benefit the refuge.

Another option is to take your own wildlife tour by following the well-marked trails. The paved Wildlife Loop is wide enough for a double stroller but short enough (about ⅓ mile) so preschoolers won't wear out. At the bird-viewing blind, even the youngest kids (with a boost from you) may peer through a slat as birds swoop within a few inches of their faces. About another 4 miles of trails, made of wood chips and other natural materials, satisfy junior and senior naturalists.

Whereas the refuge's visitor center opened in 1994, the refuge itself was established by Franklin Delano Roosevelt in 1936, the first and only unit of the National Wildlife Refuge system devoted to research. With an inquisitive child and a set of binoculars, you can undertake some research of your own here.

HEY, KIDS! Check out the visitor center's viewing pod. Here you can peer through binoculars and telescopes to see a lake where beavers build, birds (including an occasional bald eagle) soar, and Canada geese migrate—without even going outside.

KID-FRIENDLY EATS Time your visit carefully. No food or drink (except water) is allowed on the premises. If you do bring a snack or lunch, you'll have to eat it in the car. At the front desk you may request a map directing you to local fast-food restaurants, many of which are along Route 197.

PHILLIPS COLLECTION

I f you arrive by Metro, check out the Phillips Collection's poster at the Dupont Circle station. It's a good appetite whetter for this kid-comfortable museum, where you can sit back on a puffy couch or plop down on the carpet. Located in a former home—albeit a grand one—artworks are arranged in 25 galleries, 10 of which are the size of bedrooms. Six fireplaces and one fake fireplace (that looks real), in the Renoir Room, add to the museum's homey feel. Unlike most other galleries, where uniformed guards appear uninterested in the masterpieces around them, the Phillips employs art students, many of whom are artists themselves, to sit by the paintings and answer questions.

The collection's best-known painting, Renoir's *Luncheon of the Boating Party,* is particularly interesting to children because of its bright colors, the people engaged in happy conversation, and the terrier on the table. Other paintings that kids can relate to depict a ballet rehearsal, by Edgar Degas; a bullfight, by Pablo Picasso; and children playing hide-and-seek in a 19th-century house, by William Merritt Chase. The smallest gallery, devoted to works by Swiss

HEY, KIDS!
The Phillips Collection staff requests that everyone keep a safe distance—12 inches—from all paintings and sculpture, because artwork can be damaged by accident.

KEEP IN MIND The gallery's popular Family Free Days are held annually the first weekend in June, during which you can take part in projects (on a walk-in basis), which have ranged from creative collage making to key-chain making to live music. Throughout the year, three-hour, hands-on workshops for children and their parents ($10–$15 per adult/child pair) revolve around special exhibits and themes. Kids might find themselves at a photo shoot or making sculpture.

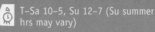
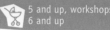
artist Paul Klee, also appeals to kids. His little paintings look as though they employ hieroglyphic symbols.

Gather a group of five or more kids (and call three weeks in advance) for a personal tour arranged around one of four themes: Art of the City, Art at Home, Picturing Performers, or Observation and Imagination. Each tour includes hands-on activities led by the museum's enthusiastic education staff. If you don't have time to book an advance tour or if the idea of being with more than a couple of kids seems daunting, you can call ahead for a family fun pack (and impress your kids with your knowledge!) or pick one up at the museum's entrance. Each pack includes artwork to discover, postcards or pictures, and activities you can try at home so the fun continues long after you've left.

KID-FRIENDLY EATS There are plenty of quick and inexpensive places to eat around Dupont Circle. For pizza, gyros, and other Greek concoctions made with tomato and cheese, try **Zorba's Cafe** (1612 20th St. NW, tel. 202/387-8555). At **Burrito Brothers** (1718 Connecticut Ave. NW, tel. 202/332-2308), kids are welcomed with coloring sheets, crayons, lollipops, and a Little Brothers meal: a small burrito filled with refried beans and cheese.

RESTON ANIMAL PARK
(SUNSHINE FARMS)

At Reston Animal Park—no longer in Reston but rather 12 miles west, in Leesburg—children get up close and personal with animals. Not only can kids talk to the animals (the parrots will even talk back), but they can also pet and feed many of them. Here domestic farm animals and exotic species live side by side. Llamas, lambs, pigs, goats, and fawns roam freely. Signs that even preschoolers can understand are posted throughout the park. Green hexagonal signs indicate that you can touch; red signs mean you can't.

Among the delights here are the antics and boisterous singing of the primates, including squirrel monkeys. Kids also enjoy kidding around with kids—baby goats, that is—who hop and jump, don't mind being petted, and love being fed. On weekends, live animal demonstrations, puppeteers, mimes, and other kids' entertainment add to the excitement.

When the park moved in 1999, Sukari the elephant moved into a breeding program, but kids can still ride ponies, go on hay rides, and enjoy dozens of other animals. Those who are too

HEY, KIDS! Here are some tips for interacting with the animals: When you feed one, keep your hand flat and your fingers together so they don't get accidentally nibbled along with the food. Only feed the animals what's sold at the park, because people food can make them sick. Also, remember not to shout, run, or tease the animals. You are guests in their home.

19270 James Monroe Hwy. (U.S. 15), Leesburg, VA

 703/759-3636

 $5 ages 2 and up

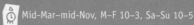 Mid-Mar–mid-Nov, M–F 10–3, Sa–Su 10–5

1–12

young to ride real animals can hop on plastic ones at the playground, where kids who want to play monkey head for the swings, slides, merry-go-round, and jungle gym. Tots who dig can break ground in the sandbox.

Birthdays are "wild" at the park, including pony rides, a live animal show, goody bags, and balloons. If you'd rather, the park will bring the zoo—four small, pettable, farmyard animals or four exotic animals, or even a customized experience—to you and your party animal.

Older kids visiting the park can earn stickers by going on scavenger hunts and completing word searches. These same kids may be concerned about the crowded conditions in some of the animal pens, but you can tell them not to be too worried. When the park closes each evening, the animals replace the children on the park's vast acreage.

KID-FRIENDLY EATS Goats eat just about anything—or at least try. Unlike goats, kids can be picky, and much of what they want their parents won't let them have. Snacks and candy are sold at the entrance. For a healthful alternative, bring a picnic or drive five minutes to the **Leesburg Restaurant** (9 S. King St., tel. 703/777–3292), in the middle of town. Locals have eaten at this dinerlike place since 1865.

KEEP IN MIND Children under 10 must be supervised at all times, and please pay attention to all the posted signs and warnings. If the sign says an animal bites, it really does. Also, watch for announcements of special events in the "Weekend" section of *The Washington Post*.

ROCK CREEK PARK

Take advantage of Rock Creek Park, the biggest stretch of parkland in Washington, offering a wealth of activities.

Take a walk *in* the wild side at the nature center, which brings the outdoors in. Pelts, bones, feathers, and a bird's nest occupy a touch table in the lobby, while another room contains stuffed animals representative of mid-Atlantic fauna. Preschoolers put on puppet shows featuring their forest friends in the Discovery Room. The center's 75-seat planetarium introduces youngsters to the solar system. Some shows include a Native American legend about a coyote who threw rocks to make pictures in the sky.

Take a hike on any of several trails near the center, but first pick up a discovery pack at the front desk for each child with you. Packs are equipped with binoculars, a field microscope, and a magnifying lens. The 15- to 20-minute Edge of the Woods trail, a flat, asphalt loop perfect for preschoolers and strollers, takes you to a pond a little larger than a bathtub,

HEY, KIDS!
If you're between the ages of 6 and 12, ask for a Junior Ranger activity book. Once you've completed at least five of the eight activities, show the book to a ranger. You will get a signed certificate and a Junior Ranger patch with a pair of raccoons on it. Display it with pride!

KEEP IN MIND The planetarium offers free weekend shows at 1 for ages 4 and up (also on Wednesday at 4) and at 4 for ages 7 and up. Children under the recommended ages may find the shows either boring or scary. (Before shows, the sun is shown setting over the Washington skyline; at the end, it rises and the room brightens.) If you skip the shows, you can still light up the sky by turning off the lights in the Discovery Room; glow-in-the-dark stickers cover the ceiling.

5200 Glover Rd. NW; stables 5100 Glover Rd. NW (between 16th St. and Connecticut Ave., south of Military Rd.)

Daily sunrise–sunset. Nature center W–Su 9–5

202/426–6829 nature center; 202/362–0117 stables

Free; pony rides $7 for 15 min; trail rides $21 per hr

2 and up, pony rides 4–7 (min 30"), trail rides 12 and up

where tadpoles swim each spring. For older children, the Woodland Trail takes 40–60 minutes, depending on how often you stop to search for animals crawling on the forest floor or chirping atop the trees. On most weekends at 2, rangers lead hikes on topics such as map and compass exploration.

Take to the saddle: Rock Creek is the only place in town where kids can become urban cowboys and cowgirls (closed-toe shoes, preferably with a small heel, required). Pony rides aren't just a trip around a circle; they're a 15-minute ride through the woods. Many preschoolers aren't ready for this excursion, but kids over 8 might find it babyish, since a teenage guide holds the reins. Before and after, kids are encouraged to pat their pony. On one-hour trail rides, guides take groups along some of the same wooded trails that Presidents Martin Van Buren and Teddy Roosevelt and World War II General George Patton once rode. After a jaunt through Rock Creek, your kids will have their own saddle stories to tell.

KID-FRIENDLY EATS Picnic areas are near the nature center. Pack a lunch from **Magruder's Grocery Store** (3627 Connecticut Ave. NW, tel. 202/237–2531), a 5- to 10-minute drive from the nature center. Near Magruder's are two inexpensive restaurants: **Bread and Chocolate** (5542 Connecticut Ave. NW, tel. 202/966–7413) and **American City Diner** (5532 Connecticut Ave. NW, tel. 202/244–1949).

ROOSEVELT ISLAND

If the wildest animal your children ever want to see is a computer mouse, Roosevelt Island isn't for your family. But for kids who believe, as Theodore Roosevelt did, that "There is delight in the hardy life of the open," this sanctuary is a superb place to get away from the city's concrete, crowds, and cars. If it weren't for the airplanes from Ronald Reagan National Airport roaring overhead, you might forget you were in D.C. altogether.

Leave your car in the parking lot next to the George Washington Memorial Parkway and walk over the bridge to this island wilderness preserve in the Potomac River. The 90-acre tribute to the conservation-minded 26th president includes 2½ miles of nature trails that crisscross marshland, swampland, and upland forest.

In the center of the island is a clearing, where a 17-foot bronze statue of Roosevelt stands, his right hand raised for emphasis. He is surrounded by shallow pools, fountains, and four large stone tablets inscribed with his thoughts on nature, manhood, state (government),

HEY, KIDS! How did the man known for the Rough Riders and carrying "a big stick" inspire a stuffed animal? Once, when Roosevelt was hunting, his aides tied up an old bear for him to kill. But he couldn't shoot the defenseless animal, which prompted a toy maker to create the teddy bear.

Off George Washington Memorial Pkwy.
northbound, near Roosevelt Bridge

 Free

 703/289-2530

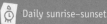 Daily sunrise–sunset

2 and up

and youth. For example, he advised students at the Groton School in Massachusetts, "Keep your eyes on the stars, but remember to keep your feet on the ground." And there is plenty of ground for your feet to cover at Roosevelt Island.

To make the most of your visit, pack a backpack with some of the following items for your children: binoculars, a magnifying glass, a sketch pad and crayons or markers, a camera, and a plant and animal guidebook, if you have one. Cattails, arrow arum, pickerelweed, willow, ash, maple, and oak all grow on the island, which is also a habitat for frogs, raccoons, birds, squirrels, and the occasional red or gray fox. But you won't see the animal most people associate with Roosevelt: the teddy bear.

KID-FRIENDLY EATS There's nothing to buy on this island—not even a soda. Since you'll be driving north on the parkway to get here, consider a stop in Georgetown first. You can pick up sandwiches, fried chicken, and salads at **Safeway** (1855 Wisconsin Ave. NW, tel. 202/333–3223). Then bring a blanket to the island, spread out near the statue, and listen to the music of birds as you eat.

KEEP IN MIND After you cross the bridge, you'll see a large bulletin board where you can pick up a trail guide. Encourage your children to stay on the marked trails. Off the trails you may encounter poison ivy and great nettles, a three-foot-tall plant better known as stinging nettles because you'll feel a stinging pain if you rub against them. Gather a group of 10 or more people and call a week in advance for a guided tour led by a park ranger, who will point out a lot more than where the stinging nettles are.

SACKLER GALLERY/FREER GALLERY OF ART

Imagine your children making an animal paperweight or sketching on a scroll while learning about ancient art techniques, geography, or other cultures. It's all part of the Freer and Sackler Galleries' ImaginAsia and ExplorAsia programs. Armed with guidebook and pencil, children (and their parents) search for textiles, sculpture, and paintings and then go beyond simply writing about what they see. They may locate on a map where a work or artist is from, interpret works, describe how they feel, or even invent stories. Afterwards, you all meet in an education room, where your kids can create a take-home craft related to the exhibits seen. These programs are operated on a drop-in basis; reservations are only required for groups of eight or more.

Even if you're not visiting on a program day, there's plenty here to interest your kids. Activity-filled guidebooks are available at each museum's information desk. And just why are there two museums, you might be wondering.

KEEP IN MIND Guidebooks list activities for a broad range of ages and abilities. Parents of young children will need to work with their kids to decide what's appropriate. Most children 10 and up can probably decide for themselves which activities are suitable.

HEY, KIDS! While you're in the Peacock Room, think about the real peacocks that used to live at the gallery. In 1993, a peacock named James and a peahen named Sylvia resided in the museum's courtyard. After one year, the gallery needed to find a new home for the birds because Sylvia laid too many eggs. Now James and Sylvia live with a farmer who loves them because they squawk to alert her when visitors arrive.

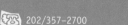
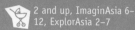

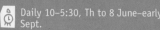
The Freer Gallery, which contains one of the world's finest collections of Asian masterpieces, was endowed by Charles Freer, who insisted on a few conditions: Objects in the collection could not be loaned out, nor could objects from outside the collection be put on display. Because of the latter, the connected Sackler Gallery was built. Like the Freer, the Sackler focuses on works from throughout Asia, but it also mounts visiting exhibits. The Freer's exhibits do change, however, but only because its permanent collection is so massive.

The Freer's collection also includes works by American artists influenced by the Orient. One such was Freer's friend James McNeil Whistler, who introduced him to Asian art. On display in Gallery 12 is Whistler's Peacock Room, a blue-and-gold *painted* dining room, decorated with painted leather, wood, and canvas and, as the name implies, devoted to peacocks. Freer paid $30,000 for the entire room and moved it from London to the United States in 1904. Perhaps your children will be influenced by the Asian masterpieces they see or inspired to decorate their bedrooms with a particular theme.

KID-FRIENDLY EATS For restaurant choices, see any of the listings for museums on the Mall: the Castle, Hirshhorn Museum and Sculpture Garden (summer only), National Air and Space Museum, National Gallery of Art, National Museum of American History, and National Museum of Natural History.

SIX FLAGS AMERICA

ashington is known for its educational and economical attractions. Six Flags America, the capital area's only theme park, isn't one of them. What it is, however, is exciting! Actually a combination theme park *and* water park (dubbed Paradise Island), it contains more than 100 rides, shows, and games spread over 150 acres in suburban Prince Georges County.

On the "dry" side, roller coaster revelers have five fast choices. The Wild One is a more than 80-year-old classic wooden coaster. Roar mixes old-fashioned wood and modern computer technology to produce a thrilling ride. The three steel coasters are the Mind Eraser, the Joker's Jinx, and the Two-Face: The Flip Side, which takes you through a 72-foot-high vertical loop—twice. Coaster traditionalists prefer the jiggle and clackety-clack sounds of the "woodie." Metal coasters follow a more circuitous route, with corkscrew turns and 360° loops. If your youngsters aren't tall enough (all rides, including the coasters, have height restrictions), head to Looney Tunes Movie Town, where even toddlers can coast on a mini-coaster, get behind the wheel of pint-size 18-wheeler, or earn their wings by flying minijets.

HEY, KIDS! It takes about a million gallons to fill up the Monsoon Lagoon—enough to fill 16,666 bathtubs. Approximately 10,000 pounds of sugar is used to make the roughly 100,000 servings of candy sold here each year—the same amount you'd use if you felt like baking nearly 1½ million chocolate chip cookies. As for hot dogs, if lined up tip to tip, the approximately 188,000 half-foot-longs sold annually would stretch the length of the Mall—about nine times.

13710 Central Ave. (Rte. 214), Largo, MD

301/249-1500

$29.99 over 48", $14.99 children 4 and up 48" and under

Early May, Sa–Su 10:30–6; mid-May–mid-June, M–F 10–6, Sa–Su 10:30–9; mid-June–Labor Day, M–F 10:30–9, Sa–Su 10:30–10

2 and up

On the "wet" side, kids like Crocodile Cal's (as in Ripkin, the Orioles star) Outback Beach House. Water-powered activities here include a barrel that dumps 1,000 gallons of water on unsuspecting passers-by every few minutes. The Monsoon Lagoon wave pool has a graduated entrance so even water babies (with parents, of course) can splash around.

Naturally everyone needs to pack swimsuits, sunscreen, and sunglasses for a fun-filled day at this entertainment complex, but parents should also bring lots of money and patience. Especially on weekends, lines begin forming even before the park opens. Most families end up spending about six to eight hours here, made easier by the availability of stroller and locker rentals. So you won't learn about American history or government. You'll still have a blast!

KID-FRIENDLY EATS No outside food is permitted, but inside is plenty of amusement park fare, like funnel cakes and cotton candy, along with beef brisket, barbecue, and crab cakes. Both the **Hollywood Backlot Café** and **Crazy Horse Saloon** are air-conditioned. Even more important than junk food to the success of a summer day, however, is water. Cups of ice sell for 25¢ at food stands.

KEEP IN MIND To maximize your chances of minimizing expenses and aggravation, prepare ahead. Look for discount coupons, or consider a season pass, which includes discounts on other parks. If your child (or your arms) needs a stroller, bring your own to save the rental fee. Discuss spending limits with your kids beforehand, not after they see things they *must* have. To avoid crowds, go on Monday or Tuesday, and make a plan upon arrival, doing what most interests your kids early. Time flies when you're having fun.

SULLY HISTORIC SITE

As at other local historic sites that recall Early American life, kids can get a real feel for how people lived two centuries ago at this museum dedicated to life in the Federal Period (1790–1820). Your children may pretend to wash dishes in an old stone sink, cool off with a folded fan, or use sugar nippers. They may soak up the scent of the green and black teas that were popular at the time or get a whiff of No. 7, a cologne that George Washington (and more recently John F. Kennedy) wore. But kids also learn that life wasn't so sweet then, and not just because the early 1800s lacked our modern amenities. Slavery, too, is addressed, and your children can handle replicas of the passes that slaves needed to leave the property or lift the heavy cast ironware slaves used in the kitchen.

Sully was the understated 1794 country home of Richard Bland Lee, uncle of Confederate general Robert E. Lee; his wife, Elizabeth Collins Lee; and their children. As Virginia's first representative to Congress, Lee cast one of two swing votes that put the nation's capital in his backyard.

KEEP IN MIND Some of the stairs are steep in the Sully mansion, so make sure that unsteady toddlers, unsteady grandparents, and distracted parents are extra careful. Strollers are not permitted in the house.

HEY, KIDS! As you look at the picture of the Lee family crest in the house, notice the squirrel on it. When the Lee children were living here, they had a pet white squirrel. One day the squirrel was let loose in the house. Imagine the excitement as the kids tried to keep their little pet from escaping outside. Can you spot the stuffed white squirrel in the parlor?

Purchase tickets and even souvenirs in a one-room, log schoolhouse that was used in nearby Haymarket during the early to mid-19th century. In this tiny room, about a half-dozen children studied under a teacher who lived above the classroom.

Guides, often Fairfax County Park Authority volunteers, conduct one-hour tours of the Lee house on the hour and half hour. Upon request, guides may tailor their talk to a child's special interest (textiles or cooking, for example) and take you to see the outbuildings and gardens. Weekends are even more festive, as Sully celebrates with such special events as soap making, kite flying, bread baking, candle making, and children's games.

After touring Sully, you may take advantage of its 127 acres. Watch as airplanes zip by or watch your own kids zip by as they run and jump on ground where children played centuries ago.

KID-FRIENDLY EATS Two cones as tall as kindergartners stand at the entrance to **Milwaukee Frozen Custard** (13934 Lee Jackson Memorial Hwy., tel. 703/263-1920). Inside, trains whiz overhead. Call in advance to see if the king of custard himself, owner Al Casey, can arrange a tour of the shop. Or visit friendly **Hunan Wok** (13635 Lee Jackson Memorial Hwy., tel. 703/968-8668).

UNITED STATES CAPITOL

Throughout the Capitol, statues, paintings, and even rooms reveal much about the people and events that shaped our nation. The frieze around the rim of the Rotunda depicts 400 years of easily recognizable American history. Columbus's arrival, the California Gold Rush, and the Wright brothers' historic flight are all here. Eight immense oil paintings depict historical scenes, four from the Revolutionary War period. See if your child can find Pocahontas in the Rotunda. (Hint: She's in three places and she doesn't resemble Disney's cartoon.)

South of the Rotunda is Statuary Hall. Here and throughout the building are statues representing each state, which your kids can search for. They range from Colorado's (and *Apollo 13*'s) Jack Swigert to Utah's Philo Farnsworth, the father of TV. Capital guides (wearing bright red) can help you locate statues.

On the north (Senate) side, you can look into the chamber once used by the Supreme Court and into the splendid Old Senate Chamber above it, both restored. In the ground-floor Brumidi

HEY, KIDS! Statuary Hall was once home to the House of Representatives (1819–1857), but some legislators back then were unhappy about one of its unusual features. Because of the perfectly spherical ceiling and sunken floor, strange things happened to sound. Echoes and "dead" spaces interfered with business. Worst of all for people with secrets, a slight whisper spoken on one side of the hall can be heard on the other. Try it! If the room isn't too noisy, the trick may work.

 East end of Mall. Metro: Capitol South or Union Station

 Free

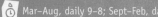 Mar–Aug, daily 9–8; Sept–Feb, daily 9–4:30

202/224–3121; 202/225–6827 guide service

 7 and up

Corridor, frescoes and oil paintings of birds, plants, American inventions, and even the *Challenger* crew adorn the walls.

As beautiful as the building is, so are the grounds, landscaped in the late-19th century by Frederick Law Olmsted, Sr. On these 68 acres you'll find the city's tamest squirrels (don't get too close; they might bite), a waterfall, and many TV news correspondents, all jockeying for position in front of the Capitol for their "stand ups." Encourage your kids to look up at the Capitol dome. The figure on top, which some might mistake for another Pocahontas, is Freedom. But the history lesson doesn't end here. Observe a session of Congress, visit your congressperson's office (hop the miniature subway in the basement to the House or Senate office building), or watch power brokers and aides in these hallowed hallways. It's the best lesson of all.

KID-FRIENDLY EATS A public **dining room** (tel. 202/224–4870), Senate-side, has served Senate bean soup, a favorite with legislators, every day since 1901. No one is sure why, though the menu outlines a few theories. The **Longworth Cafeteria** (tel. 202/225–0878), on the House side, offers several cuisines, including Mexican, Italian, and deli.

KEEP IN MIND The 30-minute guided tour is best for older kids who have studied American history. (Children younger than 10 may lose interest, because much of the narrative is about the work that takes place here rather than the building itself.) To enhance your children's appreciation, talk about Congress's role in our government before you arrive. Then during the tour, encourage them to move up front to see and hear better.

UNITED STATES HOLOCAUST
MEMORIAL MUSEUM

Like the history it covers, the Holocaust Museum can be profoundly disturbing, so you should first decide whether your children can appreciate it. The recommended ages published by the museum are guidelines only. The subject matter is complex. The museum is often crowded, making it difficult to see. The average visit is long, often two–three hours, and exhibits involve lots of reading. All that said, a trip here will be memorable for a preteen or teenager.

The museum tells the story of the 11 million Jews, Gypsies, Jehovah's Witnesses, homosexuals, political prisoners, and others killed by the Nazis between 1933 and 1945. Striving to give a you-are-there experience, the graphic presentation is as extraordinary as the subject matter: Upon arrival, each visitor is issued an "identity card" containing biographical information on a real person from the Holocaust. As you move through the museum, you read sequential updates on your card. The museum recounts the Holocaust through documentary films, videotaped and audiotaped oral histories, and a collection that includes such items as a chilling freight car, like those used to transport Jews from Warsaw to the Treblinka death camp. Although

HEY, KIDS! The doll on the second floor was made especially for a Polish Jewish girl named Zofia Burowska. Zofia kept the doll, even when she was in the Krakow ghetto, but when she was deported out of the ghetto, she gave the doll to a non-Jewish family, who saved it for her. Zofia survived, and after the war she and the doll were reunited.

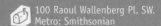

100 Raoul Wallenberg Pl. SW.
Metro: Smithsonian

202/488-0400, 800/
400-9373 ProTix

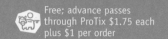
Free; advance passes
through ProTix $1.75 each
plus $1 per order

Daily 10-5:30

11 and up; Remember the
Children 8 and up

there are four privacy walls to protect visitors from especially graphic images, they don't cover all that is horrific. After this powerful experience, the adjacent Hall of Remembrance provides space for quiet reflection. If your children have further questions, take advantage of the computers in the Wexner Learning Center.

You don't need a pass for Remember the Children: Daniel's Story, an exhibit that follows one family. Children know from the beginning that Daniel survives to share his story. In this interactive exhibit, your children can follow events in Daniel's life. For example, they can see and touch the cookies in his well-stocked 1933 kitchen, but can only look at the one turnip in a pot on the stove of his 1944 ghetto apartment. At the end of the exhibit, kids are invited to write about their thoughts and feelings. It's a helpful outlet after this moving experience.

KID-FRIENDLY EATS The museum's **café,** open 8:30–4:30, offers a variety of dishes, including potato knishes, a Jewish fried or baked turnover roll.

KEEP IN MIND You will need a same-day, timed-entry pass to get into the permanent exhibition, or you can call ProTix for advance passes (fee charged). Ideally, it might be best for you to visit the museum without your children first to determine if it's appropriate. If that's not possible, consider going through Daniel's Story first. Even for teenagers, Daniel's Story will be meaningful, and you can then gauge whether to proceed.

VIETNAM VETERANS MEMORIAL

7

B e prepared for your kids to ask some serious questions about war and death after visiting this moving memorial to the 58,000 men and women who died in Vietnam. Sometimes children think all 58,000 are buried at the monument. They aren't, of course, but the slabs of black granite inscribed with the names of the dead are as somber, as powerful, and as evocative of poignant reflection as any cemetery.

Known as "the Wall," the memorial is one of the most visited sites in Washington. Conceived by Jan Scruggs, a former infantry corporal who had served in Vietnam, these black granite panels that reflect the sky, the trees, and the faces of those looking for names (and perhaps crying when they find them) was designed by Maya Ying Lin, a 21-year-old architectural student at Yale. The nontraditional war memorial was originally decried by some veterans, but with the addition of a flagpole just south of the Wall as well as Frederick Hart's statue of three soldiers, most critics were won over. When one young boy saw the statue for the first time, he exclaimed, "Look mom. They're just boys."

KID-FRIENDLY EATS Grab a hot dog or hamburger at a food kiosk behind the nearby Korean Veterans Memorial.

HEY, KIDS! You and your parents may be surprised to hear that although 10,000 women served in Vietnam, only eight women's names are on the Wall. One of these is Mary Klinker, a nurse involved in Operation Baby Lift, a mission to bring Vietnamese orphans to the United States. Klinker's plane crashed in 1975. As a memorial to these women, a stirring sculpture depicts two uniformed women caring for a wounded male soldier while a third woman kneels nearby.

Constitution Gardens, 22nd St. and Constitution Ave. NW. Metro: Foggy Bottom

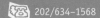 202/634–1568

 Free

24 hrs; staffed daily 8 AM–12 AM

9 and up

People's names appear on the Wall in the order of the date they died. To look up a name yourself, refer to the books posted at the entrance and exit of the memorial. But although children used to be allowed to make rubbings of names at the memorial, this practice is currently being discouraged unless you're a family member of one of the victims.

One of the most stirring aspects of the memorial are all the flowers and mementos left in remembrance, and your child may wonder what becomes of all of them. A small selection, including wedding rings, a baseball, letters, and photographs are on display on the third floor of the National Museum of American History (*see above*). Other items are stored in a warehouse in Glen Dale, Maryland, where they are fast becoming another memorial.

KEEP IN MIND Visiting the Wall might well be one of you children's most meaningful experiences in Washington, especially if you have any memories of the war or the times that you are willing to share. Giving your personal perspective, even if limited, can bring the memorial alive in a way that a drier, more historical discussion can't. Help is available from rangers, however, when your kids have questions that you can't answer.

WASHINGTON DOLLS' HOUSE & TOY MUSEUM

Some people say it's the little things in life that have the most meaning. At this quaint museum, children learn about the past from the little things that mean the most to them: dolls, toys, and games. Since this is a serious collection for doll enthusiasts, most displays are behind glass, preventing you from having to repeat, "Don't touch."

Tucked away behind Wisconsin Avenue's shopping malls, this small, yellow-brick house with a flag in front is an unexpected place for a museum celebrating the past. Purchase tickets in the front lobby at an old post office window surrounded by miniature toys in mail slots. Dollhouses are arranged in six small galleries—in some rooms from floor to ceiling—and cats lurk in almost every structure. But there's more to this museum than traditional dollhouses. Shops; stables; a one-room schoolhouse; a turn-of-the-20th-century quintet of Baltimore row houses; a 1903 New Jersey seaside hotel; and an elaborate Mexican house with an aviary, a working elevator, and a garage with a vintage automobile help youngsters appreciate how people lived in different places and at different times.

HEY, KIDS! Have you ever tried to make a house out of paper? It's harder than it looks. In 1884, when Gertrude Horsey Smith (yes, that was her middle name) was about 12, she made a paper house. You can see this house in the lobby of the museum. Be sure to turn the table around to see the back of the house, so you can look at the paper piano, dining room set, and more.

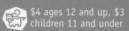
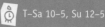
Antique toys and games include an Old Maid card game, circus performers and animals, dominoes the size of a child's fingernails, and many tea sets. Noah's arks and animals are examples of "Sunday toys," which children could only play with on Sundays in some religious families. Imagine keeping Sunday's toys separate from Monday's these days!

Pastimes such as baseball and holidays are observed with special exhibits. Come at Christmas and you'll see a revolving musical tree. During February, you'll see Victorian Valentines. You can even celebrate your child's own holiday—his birthday—with a party in the museum's Edwardian tea room.

After going through the museum, your little ones might want to visit the museum's shops. One is dedicated to dollhouse furniture and accessories for collectors; the other carries kid-friendly merchandise.

KEEP IN MIND If you're child gets bored and needs a little action, talk to a member of the museum's staff. They will accommodate requests to send a 1930s Lionel train whizzing and whistling around its tracks. Kids can also pull a string to ring the bell at an old Ohio schoolhouse.

KID-FRIENDLY EATS A block up Jenifer Street from the museum is **Booeymonger** (5252A Wisconsin Ave. NW, tel. 202/686–5805), known for creative sandwiches, and **T.G.I. Friday's** (5252B Wisconsin Ave. NW, tel. 202/237–1880), where you can get a meal and a sundae. Or, try **McDonald's** (5300 Wisconsin Ave. NW, tel. 202/244–1122), on the lower level of the nearby Mazza Gallerie.

WASHINGTON MONUMENT

This 555'5" obelisk (10 times as tall as its width at the base) punctuates the capital like a huge, partially buried exclamation point. Visible from nearly everywhere in the city, it serves as a landmark for visiting tourists and lost motorists alike and a beacon for anyone who yearns to shoot to the top and survey all of Washington below.

A limited number of free tickets, good for a half-hour period, are available at the kiosk on 15th Street beginning at 7:30 April–Labor Day and 8:30 the rest of the year. Advance tickets are available from Ticketmaster.

Arrive at the monument at the allotted time. Although lines to get in may be long, they move quickly. If your children are restless, have them count the flags surrounding the monument. (There are 50: one for each state.) Once you're inside, an elevator whizzes to the top in just 65 seconds. There you may enjoy a bird's-eye view of the city for as long as you like.

KID-FRIENDLY EATS A refreshment stand at the bottom of the hill sells ice cream in the summer and hot chocolate in the winter as well as sandwiches. For some down-to-earth good food, try a restaurant at the United States Holocaust Memorial Museum or the National Museum of American History (*see above*).

HEY, KIDS! It took over 50 years to build this monument. Fund-raising began in 1833, and the cornerstone was laid in 1848. By the Civil War, construction had stopped. (Look for a ring about a third of the way up; the marble used to complete the monument later was of a slightly different shade.) Cattle roamed and Union troops were trained here. Finally completed in 1884, it was the world's tallest structure. Four years later it was opened to visitors, but only men could ride the elevator—considered too dangerous for women, who had to climb the stairs if they wanted to see the view.

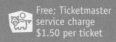

15th St. and Constitution Ave.
NW. Metro: Smithsonian

202/426-6841;
202/432-7328 Ticketmaster

Free; Ticketmaster
service charge
$1.50 per ticket

Apr–Labor Day, daily 8 AM–12 AM,
early Sept–Mar, daily 9–5

5 and up

Each of the four sides has two viewing stations, and every other station is equipped with a step. Small children may think Washington looks like Legoland. Older children may enjoy trying to find Washington's landmarks. (A street map, available in the gift shop, is helpful for this). On a very clear day, you can see Shenandoah National Park to the west. On a clear night, you can spy the flame by John F. Kennedy's grave in Arlington National Cemetery (*see above*). A National Park Service ranger stationed at the top can answer any questions.

When you're ready to land, descend one flight of stairs to the elevator. This level also houses a small bookshop that carries a modest selection of children's books about Washington the place and Washington the man.

Though closed for restoration and the creation of new exhibits, the monument is due to reopen by July 4, 2000. While it's closed, you can visit the interactive Interpretive Center, where a viewing room re-creates the panoramas from up top.

KEEP IN MIND Judging by the crowds, it seems there are as many people who want to look down on the Washington action literally as there are those who look down on it figuratively. If you don't want to wait in line or the monument is still closed, you have other options: Washington National Cathedral's Pilgrim Observation Gallery (*see below*) and the Old Post Office Pavilion (*see the J. Edgar Hoover FBI Building*) both offer awesome views.

WASHINGTON NATIONAL CATHEDRAL

Boys and girls go Gothic at this, the sixth-largest cathedral in the world. Like its 14th-century counterparts, the National Cathedral (officially Washington's Cathedral Church of St. Peter and St. Paul) has a nave, flying buttresses, and vaults that were built stone by stone. Fanciful gargoyles adorn the outside of the building. Inside, a stained-glass window with an encapsulated moon rock celebrates the Apollo 11 space flight, and statues of George Washington and Abraham Lincoln stand as tributes. Pick up a children's guide to the cathedral at the front door or at the Medieval Workshop in the cathedral's crypt.

Aside from seeing the cathedral itself, however, there are lots of other activities for kids. At Medieval Workshops (given Saturdays as well as summer weekdays), your children can create a clay gargoyle, carve limestone, piece together a stained-glass window, and make a brass rubbing while learning about life in the Middle Ages. Workshops aren't drop-off affairs, though; those under 12 must be accompanied by an adult. Keep in mind that if you're also with children younger than five there's little in the crypt to entertain them.

HEY, KIDS! At the east side of St. Peter's tower, almost at the top, is a stone grotesque of Darth Vader, a model of which is in the Medieval Workshop. A 13-year-old boy won a contest to design a decorative sculpture for the cathedral. Bring binoculars. They make Vader—and a lot of the other gargoyles—easier to spot.

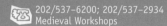
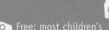
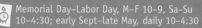
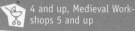
On Family Saturdays, children 4–9 explore the nooks and crannies of the cathedral before making such crafts as stained-glass-like pinwheels, shields, kaleidoscopes, and mosaics. During the very popular family gargoyle tours, children see a slide show on these creepy critters, hear stories about their creation, and then get an up-close encounter with a few of them. Also of interest to young and old, the Pilgrim Observation Gallery provides a panoramic view of Washington. A charming children's chapel with kneelers depicts the story of Noah's ark, outside in the Bishop's Garden is a maze, and a greenhouse contains exotic herbs and even a few bug-eating plants.

Going to church has probably never been so varied and so fun.

KEEP IN MIND

While the cathedral is a cool place for kids, it still is a house of worship, so encourage your children to be as quiet as church mice in the main church and chapels. If they just need to run around and let off steam, you can take them to the Bishop's Garden, ideal for a game of hide-and-seek.

KID-FRIENDLY EATS The only place to get something to eat on the cathedral grounds is the **museum shop** (tel. 202/537–6267), which has sandwiches and yogurt in a self-serve refrigerator. The cathedral is surrounded by green gardens that are great for a picnic, however. A few blocks north you'll find **Cactus Cantina** (3300 Wisconsin Ave. NW, tel. 202/686–7222), a lively Mexican restaurant, and **Cafe Deluxe** (3228 Wisconsin Ave. NW, tel. 202/686–2233), which includes a three-vegetable entrée among its children's offerings.

WHEATON REGIONAL PARK

3

A ll aboard! A little red replica of an 1863 train chugs along on 10-minute tours through the woods at this park within 10 miles of D.C. But there's more for children here than just choo-choo rides.

Your youngsters can whiz around on a carousel, ride a life-size statue of a camel, or peer over the turrets of a castle, conveniently located in a sandbox that can accommodate a whole class of kids. The playground is packed with bouncing wooden bridges, ladders, swings, mazes, wooden jeeps with bright plastic steering wheels, and straight and spiral slides in all sizes— from less than 6 feet long to more than 60 feet long.

Facilities for sports lovers include hiking trails, an ice rink, tennis courts, baseball fields, and volleyball courts. The Brookside Nature Center offers dozens of free and low-cost nature programs throughout the year, including hikes, puppet shows, workshops, and summer camps, but even without a special program, the nature center is a fun place to visit. Kids can

KID-FRIENDLY EATS The train station has a **snack bar** (tel. 301/946–6396) open daily during summer, when the ice cream it sells is a welcome treat. Picnic tables are available. **Wheaton Plaza** (11160 Viers Mill Rd., tel. 301/946–3200), about 3 miles away, has a food court.

KEEP IN MIND If you're closer to the Potomac, you might prefer 500-acre Cabin John Regional Park (7400 Tuckerman La., Rockville, MD, tel. 301/299–0024). Facilities here include the Locust Grove Nature Center (7777 Democracy Blvd., North Bethesda, tel. 301/299–1990) and a train replica. Your child can pretend to ride Cinderella's pumpkin coach or watch the Bethesda Big Train (tel. 301/983–1006) play in a summer baseball league. Feed trash to the talking pig near the train station.

2000 Shorefield Rd., Wheaton, MD; nature center: 1400 Glenallan Ave.; gardens: 1800 Glenallan Ave.

 Daily sunrise–sunset; some attractions seasonal

 301/946–7033; 301/946–9071 nature center; 301/949–8230 gardens

Free; some attractions extra

 6 mth and up

check out live snakes, fish, and turtles; play nature games on the computer; and put puzzles together.

Next to the nature center is Brookside Gardens, where formal seasonal displays of bulbs, annuals, perennials, and a sprawling azalea garden flourish outside and seasonal displays and exotic tropicals blossom inside. The garden's annual children's day, held the last Saturday in September, features sing-alongs, crafts and games. During the winter, take a stroll through Brookside's Garden of Lights. You won't see Santa or a menorah at this secular presentation, but you will see bears, owls, squirrels, cherry trees, and black-eyed Susans—all lit up brighter than stars to enchant children of all ages.

HEY, KIDS! Try finding the queen bee in the beehive at the Brookside Nature Center. (It's even trickier than finding Waldo, because all the bees are moving.) Beekeepers put a dot on her back, and she's slightly bigger than the hundreds of other honeybees swarming around behind glass. You can get within ½" of them and not get stung! You can also watch the bees move freely between their home in the nature center and the outdoors.

WHITE HOUSE

I f you think about it, it's really rather extraordinary that our president opens his house most mornings to throngs of visitors who peer past ropes at his family's dining and living rooms.

There are two ways to visit the White House. The most popular (and easiest) way is to pick up timed tickets, dispensed on a first-come, first-served basis at the White House Visitor Center. During the busy spring and summer seasons, however, if you're not in line by 6 AM, you may be out of luck. (Maybe it's not so easy after all.) If you do rise early enough to get a ticket, it'll tell you where and when your tour begins. Plan on arriving 5–10 minutes early. Tours don't include guides, which may be just as well for small children. Secret Service agents stationed in each room will answer your questions.

The other option is to write to your representative or senator's office 8–10 weeks in advance to request special VIP passes for a guided tour between 8 and 10 AM. These tickets are extremely

HEY, KIDS! Are you ready to roll? And do you have a younger brother or sister? If you do, you might be able to roll Easter eggs on the White House lawn Easter Monday, as kids have done since the 1800s. Just as with the White House tour, the Easter egg roll involves waiting in line, but it's cool enough to be worth the wait. Adults (and big kids!), however, must be accompanied by a young child (aged 3–6 or thereabouts).

limited. Both tours last about 20–25 minutes and take you through the East Room (where Teddy Roosevelt allowed his children to ride a pony), the Green Room, the Blue Room, the Red Room, and the State Dining Room.

Many children hope to see the president or at least a presidential pet. The chances of glimpsing either are nil, but your youngsters can look for inanimate animals on the tour. For example, a couch in the Red Room has dolphins on its legs. All the Great Seals depict a bald eagle, whose head is turned either toward olive branches, representing peace, or toward arrows, signifying a time of war. If your children are disappointed that they didn't get to chat with the president or want to tell him that it's time to change the color scheme of his house, they may write him. He even has his own zip code: 20501. So does the First Lady; hers is 20502.

KID-FRIENDLY EATS At popular **Old Ebbitt Grill** (675 15th St. NW, tel. 202/347–4800), parents like the homemade pasta, and kids appreciate the goodies accompanying their meals. **The Shops** (National Press Building, F and G Sts. between 13th and 14th Sts. NW, tel. 202/662–7000) houses a food hall and restaurants, such as the **Boston Seafood Company** (tel. 202/737–9211).

KEEP IN MIND One thing to remember about the White House tour is that the older your kids are, the more they can appreciate. A more practical consideration for parents of young children is that there are no public rest rooms in the White House. The closest ones are in the Ellipse Visitor Pavilion (where tours assemble) and in the White House Visitor Center, across 15th Street. The visitor center has a whole section devoted to the families who have lived in the White House.

WOLF TRAP FARM PARK FOR THE
PERFORMING ARTS

Over a stream and through the woods, you'll find a clearing with benches and a stage where the National Park Service sponsors Theatre-in-the-Woods for 7–10 weeks every summer (depending on funding). Though this venue is most often associated with adult concerts, as many as 1,000 people per performance come here to see professional children's performers, such as jugglers, musicians, clowns, and puppeteers. Sometimes a former Harlem Globetrotter shows off his basketball artistry and antics.

Afterward, romping through the park is encouraged. Children (and parents!) roll down the grassy hill, skip stones or wade in the stream, and picnic in the meadow under shady trees. Sometimes park rangers give impromptu nature tours.

For one weekend in September, Wolf Trap hosts the International Children's Festival, which features performers, crafts, and music from other countries. If your kids are too young to know about countries, they're probably familiar with streets, especially the one called

KEEP IN MIND On Tuesday, Thursday, and Saturday after the 10 o'clock shows, performers stay for about 40 minutes to teach workshops for children 4 and up. Groups of about 30–40 kids gain insight into the performing arts, such as proper clown etiquette or simple ballet techniques or mime moves. Reservations aren't required for performances, but they're a must for the free workshops.

Sesame. Bob McGrath ("Bob" on "Sesame Street") and at least one other character from this famous thoroughfare perform each year. Three stages—the Theatre-in-the-Woods, the Meadow Pavilion, and the Filene Center (a covered amphitheater)—feature entertainment from puppet shows to clowns. Though face painting is offered, kids can't choose the usual animal or flower. They must select a flag from one of the countries celebrated or a U.S. flag. One of the most popular festival areas is the Arts/Technology Pavilion; here kids draw posters that are scanned by computer, dance for video cameras, and learn about the future through computers.

Everything except food is included in the price. If it rains, everything moves to tents and the Filene Center. Hopefully that won't dampen spirits too much.

KID-FRIENDLY EATS No food or drink (except water) is permitted in the theater, because of bees. If you want to bring food, you'll have to leave it, securely wrapped, at a picnic table during a show. Ten minutes away at the **Rainforest Café** (1961 Chain Bridge Rd., Fairfax, tel. 703/821–1900), in the Tyson's Corner Shopping Center, animated wildlife, waterfalls, and other special effects entertain diners.

HEY, KIDS! Were you wondering why this facility is called Wolf Trap Farm Park? During Colonial times, this area was covered in farms. Wolves were considered a danger to livestock, and farmers would reward anyone who could trap the creatures. There haven't been any wolves here for a long time, but you may spot deer, foxes, or groundhogs.

games

THE CLASSICS

"I'M THINKING OF AN ANIMAL..." With older kids you can play 20 Questions: Have your leader think of an animal, vegetable, or mineral (or, alternatively, a person, place, or thing) and let everybody else try to guess what it is. The correct guesser takes over as leader. If no one figures out the secret within 20 questions, the first person goes again. With younger children, limit the guessing to animals and don't put a ceiling on how many questions can be asked. With rivalrous siblings, just take turns being leader. Make the game's theme things you expect to see at your day's destination.

"I SEE SOMETHING YOU DON'T SEE AND IT IS BLUE."
Stuck for a way to get your youngsters to settle down in a museum? Sit them down on a bench in the middle of a room and play this vintage favorite. The leader gives just one clue—the color—and everybody guesses away.

FUN WITH THE ALPHABET

"I'M GOING TO THE GROCERY..." The first player begins, "I'm going to the grocery and I'm going to buy... " and finishes the sentence with the name of an object, found in grocery stores, that begins with the letter "A". The second player repeats what the first player has said, and adds the name of another item that starts with "B". The third player repeats everything that has been said so far and adds something that begins with "C" and so on through the alphabet. Anyone who skips or misremembers an item is out (or decide up front that you'll give hints to all who need 'em). You can modify the theme depending on where you're going that day, as "I'm going to X and I'm going to see..."

"I'M GOING TO ASIA ON AN ANT TO ACT UP." Working their way through the alphabet, players concoct silly sentences stating where they're going, how they're traveling, and what they'll do.

FAMILY ARK   Noah had his ark—here's your chance to build your own. It's easy: Just start naming animals and work your way through the alphabet, from antelope to zebra.

WHAT I SEE, FROM A TO Z   In this game, kids look for objects in alphabetical order—first something whose name begins with "A", next an item whose name begins with "B", and so on. If you're in the car, have children do their spotting through their own window. Whoever gets to Z first wins. Or have each child play to beat his own time. Try this one as you make your way through zoos and museums, too.

games

JUMP-START A CONVERSATION

games

WHAT IF...? Riding in the car and waiting in a restaurant are great times to get to know your youngsters better. Begin with imaginative questions to prime the pump.

• If you were the tallest man on earth, what would your life be like? The shortest?
• If you had a magic carpet, where would you go? Why? What would you do there?
• If your parents gave you three wishes, what would they be?
• If you were elected president, what changes would you make?
• What animal would you like to be and what would your life be like?
• What's a friend? Who are your best friends? What do you like to do together?
• Describe a day in your life 10 years from now.

DRUTHERS How do your kids really feel about things? Just ask. "Would you rather eat worms or hamburgers? Hamburgers or candy?" Choose serious and silly topics—and have fun!

FAKER, FAKER Reveal three facts about yourself. The catch: One of the facts is a fake. Have your kids ferret out the fiction. Take turns being the faker. Fakers who stump everyone win.

KEEP A STRAIGHT FACE

"HA!" Work your way around the car. First person says "Ha." Second person says "Ha, ha." Third person says "Ha" three times. And so on. Just try to keep a straight face. Or substitute "Here, kitty, kitty, kitty!"

WIGGLE & GIGGLE Give your kids a chance to stick out their tongues at you. Start by making a face, then have the next person imitate you and add a gesture of his own—snapping fingers, winking, clapping, sneezing, or the like. The next person mimics the first two and adds a third gesture, and so on.

JUNIOR OPERA During a designated period of time, have your kids sing everything they want to say.

IGPAY ATINLAY Proclaim the next 30 minutes Pig Latin time, and everybody has to talk in this fun code. To speak it, move the first consonant of every word to the end of the word and add "ay." "Pig" becomes "igpay," and "Latin" becomes "atinlay." To words that being with a vowel, just add "ay" as a suffix.

MORE GOOD TIMES

BUILD A STORY "Once upon a time there lived..." Finish the sentence and ask the rest of your family, one at a time, to add another sentence or two. Bring a tape recorder along to record the narrative—and you can enjoy your creation again and again.

NOT THE GOOFY GAME Have one child name a category. (Some ideas: first names, last names, animals, countries, friends, feelings, foods, hot or cold things, clothing.) Then take turns naming things that fall into that category. You're out if you name something that doesn't belong in the category—or if you can't think of another item to name. When only one person remains, start again. Choose categories depending on where you're going or where you've been—historic topics if you've seen a historic sight, animal topics before or after the zoo, upside-down things if you've been to the circus, and so on. Make the game harder by choosing category items in A-B-C order.

COLOR OF THE DAY Choose a color at the beginning of your outing and have your kids be on the lookout for things that are that color, calling out what they've seen when they spot it. If you want to keep score, keep a running list or use a pen to mark points on your kids' hands for every item they spot.

CLICK If Cam Jansen, the heroine of a popular series of early-reader books, says "Click" as she looks at something, she can remember every detail of what she sees, like a camera (that's how she got her nickname). Say "Click!" Then give each one of your kids a full minute to study a page of a magazine. After everyone has had a turn, go around the car naming items from the page. Players who can't name an item or who make a mistake are out.

THE QUIET GAME Need a good giggle—or a moment of calm to figure out your route? The driver sets a time limit and everybody must be silent. The last person to make a sound wins.

THEMATIC INDEX

ACKNOWLEDGMENTS

This book is dedicated with appreciation to the Smithsonian Institution employees and volunteers, the National Park Service rangers, and all the museum guides, naturalists, and docents who make Washington such an enriching environment for children. Thank you also to my editor, Andrea Lehman at Fodor's, for her wit and wisdom. On a personal note, I am grateful to my mother and husband for their encouragement and to Norman and Timmy for helping me to witness Washington's wonders through the eyes of a child.

–Kathryn McKay

the end